Mangia Strong

The recipes and stories of my Italian family

by
Linda Zilioli Vanderbeck

To my Mom,

Nonna Crocco, Nonna Zilioli and

my Aunt Teresa and Aunt Louise -

the women whose hands prepared the many meals and dinners

that inspired this book.

CONTENTS

Introduction

Greeting

As far as I am concerned one of the greatest joys in life is sharing good food with people I love and care about. I find comfort in the warmth and security that surround a kitchen busied with the preparation of a meal for loved ones. In my vocabulary "let's get together" and "let's eat" are nearly synonymous. I fill much of my life with the preparation and enjoyment of food because food and eating touch me at the very heart of my primeval sense of life. If I sound a bit fanatical it's probably because I am.

During my childhood, family experiences always involved food in some way and is probably where my interest in cooking and eating has stemmed.

My love for cooking and eating has motivated me to write this book so that the many wonderful foods that my family has given to me can be shared and preserved.

So in the words my Nonno Crocco said as we sat down to eat...

Mangia Strong

Growing Up Italian

I grew up in an Italian family which has molded my life and left me with many treasured memories. When I think of our family life, I remember dinners on Sunday (or any other occasion for that matter), delicious foods and playing with my cousins. The women usually spent most of the day in and about the kitchen cooking, cleaning and enjoying one another's company. The men played cards, bocci or watched whatever major sporting event was being televised that day. And we kids, well we were kids. We were never discouraged from helping in the kitchen but instead were encouraged and sometimes required to participate. I am sure that my interest and love for cooking are rooted in these childhood experiences.

Family dinners were eaten at the dining room table in one of my nonne's home or in my mother's or one of my aunt's basement. (We always called our grandmothers Nonna, which means grandmother in Italian. Our grandfathers

were Nonno.) Each household in my family, in addition to having two kitchens, has acquired for the specific purpose of hosting a family dinner, several large folding tables, numerous folding chairs and table service for twenty-four. My mother owned a 30-cup coffee maker which was shared with my aunts. The tables were set in a line, covered with table cloths and beautifully set and decorated. The table setting was not exactly formal, but attractive and tasteful. Usually plates of vegetables with cold cuts, bowls of olives and baskets of crusty bread were placed on the tables for appetizers. Once beverages were offered another wonderful family dinner was on its way.

When I was in my twenties I moved away from home and spent holidays with my friends' families. It was not until then that I realized not all families are like mine. I was quite surprised when at a friend's family dinner we were required to find places to sit wherever we could, which may or may not have been at the table. Some of us had to sit in the living room with our plates on our laps or on TV trays. I remember thinking, "why didn't they set up the folding tables and chairs?", when it occurred to me that they didn't have any! This is probably the point in my life when I started to appreciate the unique family experience I had been given.

Family dinners were food extravaganzas because eating and sharing food is central to Italian culture. Even a simple evening visit to either one of my nonne was sure to include food. Within 5-minutes of entering my nonna's home, she would begin brewing a pot of coffee (to this day this phenomenon will occur in any one of my family member's home.) To accompany the coffee there were always cookies, cakes and/or breads. As children we were often allowed to have coffee with the adults which I remember as a special treat. My nonna would give us a cup of equal parts milk and coffee and allow us to add sugar. In the fall Nonna Margherita would roast chestnuts, or castagne as we called them, and would bring them to the table wrapped in a damp cloth. As she unwrapped them, the warm steam would fill the room with their sweet, woodsy aroma. We would all sit around the table and visit while we ate the nuts.

During a visit to my Nonna Crocco while in my teens, I really didn't want anything so refused all of her offers of food and beverage. As we were leaving, I hugged her and thanked her for her hospitality and was taken aback when she responded with genuinely bruised feelings because I had eaten nothing. It was then that I realized the offering of food is not merely an attempt to satisfy a visitor's hunger, but is a gesture of love and kinship. It is a ritual where bonds and relationships are cemented and to refuse the offer is to reject the affection being extended. Since that evening, I have never refused to eat while visiting her.

The association of food in the Italian culture is more subtly demonstrated in the vegetable garden. My parents, nonne and nonni and aunts-and-uncles have always had lovely vegetable gardens in their backyards. As a child I remember my nonne-and-nonni's yards being nearly all garden. As spring approached, attention and energy was devoted to preparing and planting the garden. The summer was filled with caring and nurturing to be followed by the harvest in late summer and fall. For some reason, the tomato plants seemed to have aristocratic status as far as garden vegetables go. It is as if the purpose of the garden was to grow tomatoes and growing the other vegetables was superfluous. My Nonno Louie would start his tomato plants from seeds which were produced by the previous season's most promising tomato plants. He built a bottomless wooden frame about 2-feet by 4-feet with a hinged glass cover which he set over a special area of the garden devoted to tomato seed gemination. The glass covering served as a mini greenhouse and the hinged cover allowed him to control the temperature by propping up the cover on warm days. Nonno Natale watered his tomatoes with sun-warmed rain water he collected in large wooden tubs from the down spouts which, according to him, is in part responsible for the beautiful tomatoes he produced. From these gardens we ate wonderful fresh salads and delicious vegetable dinners.

Of course, Italian culture encompasses much more than food and eating. Yet, the thought and taste of the many delicious foods we ate will always invoke in me the sense of love, caring and loyalty that is so willingly given by my family.

My Nonne's Kitchens

The home kitchen has always been the family epicenter whether it be a week-day meal, huge family dinner party, or anything in between. People tend to gravitate to the kitchen where conversation, laughter, a peek into a simmering pot on the stove, and maybe a wine or two seem to create a special uniting affect that for whatever reason, doesn't happen in the other rooms of the house. It seems that it's during these times spent in the kitchen together, that the bonds and loyalties we have with one another are forged. And to think, generations ago in the small farming villages of Casnigo and Falerna, my Nonne's kitchens, undecorated and austere, held this same charisma.

Nonna Zilioli's Kitchen in Casnigo, Bergamo

Nonna's kitchen was long and narrow. In the middle sat a large table. At one end was a fireplace with a seat to one side where she prepared the family meals. Copper and cast iron pots were held over the fire by hooks at the end of long swinging arms. Skillets sat on tripods and since there was no oven, roasting was done in a large pan. The pots and pans were cleaned with salt, vinegar and cornmeal and those with handles when not being used, hung on hooks over the fireplace. Most of the cooking utensils were wooden. An artesian well provided plenty of "sweet" water.

Nonna's typical day would start by building a fire in the fireplace and cooking a soft polenta with milk for the morning's breakfast. Because Bergamo is in the foothills of the Alps, it was ideal for raising dairy cows (Nonna had two) so naturally, dairy products formed the basis for much of the cuisine. Milk was stored in large shallow pans in the coolest room of the house which was generally the root cellar. The cream was scooped off the top with a large wooden bowl and turned into butter. The remaining milk was made into cheese by transferring it to a large kettle and adding a piece of caccio. Caccio was the fermented milk from a young animal's stomach which turned the milk into curd. (In later years, Nonna bought rennet to start the cheese making process). Nonna used a wooden branch to break up the curd before it was placed into forms and drained. Over time the cheese aged and hardened.

The best cheeses were made during the summer when milk could not stand in the warm weather long enough for the cream to be collected. If there was any extra milk, Nonna used it to make soup like pasta or polenta col lach. Stracchino was a cream-rich cheese and fumicato was a cheese aged in sacks near the fireplace. The whey that was left behind after the curd was removed was turned into ricotta by heating and adding a bit more caccio.

Nonna's meals also included seasonal vegetables from her garden like potatoes, cabbage, radicchio, green beans and beets. She used the savory herbs she grew (sage, rosemary and parsley) and the spices she bought (nutmeg, clove and pepper) to season her dishes.

Of course, Nonna made many polente - the staple of the Bergamese diet. Nonna grew corn that was taken to the miller weighed out in kilos. He would grind the corn with a mill stone turned by an electric motor and return the millings separated in sacks of cornmeal and bran. The bran was mixed with whey and fed to the chickens and pigs.

On most days, Nonna also prepared minestra - a bland soup of water flavored with only a small amount of finely chopped pancetta or bit of butter into which a few strands of homemade fettuccine were cooked. Despite the minestra being topped with grated cheese and in summer, enriched with a few legumes, Aunt Teresa and my dad hated this soup. Nonna was a very frugal cook and although could have used some eggs in her fettuccine or a chicken in her broth, she never did. She even told a joke about a person that used bones in their minestra and afterwards loaned them to a neighbor for their minestra.

Pane cotto was another lunchtime soup consisting of dry bread cooked in water and butter then topped with cheese. This soup was commonly fed to babies, the elderly, and people who were sick. An extravagant version of pane cotto included a beaten egg cooked in the broth.

The mountains surrounding Bergamo produced an abundance of chestnut trees so Nonna and her family would gather the nuts for winter. The chestnuts stored well and were either roasted or boiled and were also served to guests.

Fresh fish was a rarity except for the occasional small "pescilli" that came from a neighboring town (Uncle Lino's hometown) where there was a lake. Otherwise, fish consisted of baccala, dried-salted herring and sardines, or the occasional canned tuna.

Like today, special foods were associated with specific holidays. In February, Nonna and her family celebrated Mardi Gras with gnocchi and saltasu for dessert. For Easter she made a plain cookie that she cut into strips and took to the local baker to cook in his oven. August 5th hailed a regional holiday that paid homage to Madona D'Erbia, the patron saint of Casnigo (the town in Bergamo where Nonna lived). Everyone traveled up to the mountains where the Arch Bishop of Bergamo would say mass. The holiday was celebrated with a fair where a shaved ice (probably saved snow) flavored with a grenadine like syrup was sold. Panettone, sometimes shaped like a wreath, also typified the holiday.

Nonna Crocco's Kitchen in Falerna, Calabria

Nonna's kitchen was on the first floor of the house where the cooking was done on a fireplace. Firewood was stored in a shack outside, and every few days wood was carried from the shack and stacked near the fireplace. Cooking was done in pots on tripods or hanging from hooks over the fire. Bread was not baked in the house but instead in a wood-fire oven that was outside near the stable.

Next to the fireplace was a credenza that held an assortment of pantry items that included bread, tomato paste and dishes. A table sat in the middle of the room. On one of the walls was a shelf with curved racks made to hold barrels of water on their side. In this orientation, one had to merely turn the barrel to pour the water. Under these racks was a trap door through which dish washing water was drained, mixed with bran, and fed to the pigs. Drinking water was kept in terra cotta jugs.

Another area of the kitchen held two large bins covered by a hinged lid. Each was divided into three equal sized compartments that held frize, figs and flour. Next to the stairway was a loom on which Nonna's mother, Letizia Giudice Menniti, worked each morning before everyone else was awake. Outside of the house was a stable area that housed the milk goat, the fattened pigs and the pack mule.

Nonna and her family produced nearly all their food by farming their ten properties. Each property had a unique name that the family used to refer to its location and use.
- *Marina* - vineyard and fig trees
- *Lupia* - vegetables - tomatoes, eggplant, peppers and beans
- *Carulie* - vineyard and a few fruit trees including pears
- *Rinelda* - large olive orchard and two story shed for storing hay and feed for the animals

- *Guartu dei Palacchiagi* - winter cabbage - this was a small plot at the end of town that was somewhat sheltered from freezing
- *Stia* - potatoes
- *Havali* - olive trees and a few orange trees - this property belonged to Nonno Crocco
- *Monache* - castagne, legumes that were dried for winter, and potatoes
- *Niapute* - beans and potatoes
- *Luartu de Vaggune* - uncommon red-fruited fig trees - was a small patch of land

There was essentially no mechanization so everything was done by hand. After working all season to produce a crop of roma (or San Marzano) tomatoes, Nonna spent several days converting them into tomato paste for winter storage. The tomatoes were washed, cut and simmered in their own juices. They were then cooled and forced through a wooden-sided sieve into a bowl. The strained sauce was further cooked until thick, and then finished with some salt. When cool, the paste was spread about 2" thick on sieve bottomed, stainless steel pans and left in the sun for about two days while being periodically turned, in order to evaporate off excess water. The resulting tomato paste was transferred to small crocks and covered with a couple inches of olive oil. A spicy version was made from a portion of the tomato paste by adding hot peppers.

Many vegetables, especially zucchini and eggplant, were dried or preserved in crocks of oil and spices. Olives and pimentos were sometimes pickled with vinegar. Legumes like white beans, roma beans, small red beans, fava beans, garbanzo beans, and peas were also dried and saved for winter. Figs were dried and packed in bins to be eaten for lunches with a piece of bread. Chestnuts (castagna) were also stored and eaten during the winter.

An important food source for Nonna and her family were the two pigs that her father (Giovanni Menniti) butchered each winter. Each October during the Festival of Madonna del Rosario, he bought two piglets that would be contributing to the family's larder the winter of the year after next. These animals provided an array of sausages, salami, prosciutto and capocollo that were smoked for several weeks with olive pits and skins left from the olive oil making process. After smoking, some were hung in the attic to further cure into a pepperoni-like sausage. One variety of sausage was made from the internal organs and another was only partially smoked and then put in crocks and covered with melted lard that had been rendered from the pigs' fat. Even the blood clods were fried with onions and the blood was cooked in a double boiler with wine syrup, sugar, chocolate, raisins, orange peel and walnuts.

Contributing to the deliciousness of these pork products was the pigs' varied and nutritious diet. They ate chestnuts, bran, prickly pears and a small fava bean that was grown especially for them. In the fall before the slaughter, they feasted on a boiled mixture of figs, pumpkins and potatoes.

Christmas Eve was the major holiday that Nonna and her family celebrated with a hearty meal of fried baccala and pasta aglia e olio. Dinner was followed by nuts and oranges and usually a batch of cuddurieddi. On Christmas day, the family splurged with a fresh meat sugo that they made from a piece of kid or mutton. Easter was celebrated with fragoni, gudzupe, lard bread and pigno-lata.

Appetizers

Antipasto

My mom, aunts and Nonne were not lavish hostesses but more often then not, upon arrival to their homes for dinner, and before sitting down to eat, their guests were welcomed with platters and bowls brimming with antipasto.

An ever present traditional antipasto, included platters of attractively arranged meats and cheeses along side marinated vegetables and olives. Baskets of crusty Italian bread and crunchy breadsticks were never far away. Pitted black olives were commonly included which we kids enjoyed stuffed with the tips of our fingers and eaten from one finger at a time.

The countless combinations of meats, cheeses and vegetables offer limitless possibilities for this dish. With the popularization of ethnic foods in mainstream grocery stores, it should be easy to find authentic ingredients but certainly seek out your local Italian grocer. Offer a variety, and adjust the amounts based on the number of people you are serving. Be sure to keep the portions modest as your guests will find it hard to stop indulging on this delicious appetizer and might otherwise not have room for dinner.

Select an assortment allowing 2-4 oz. meats and/or cheeses plus ¼-⅓ c. vegetables per person. Without exception, have the meats sliced thin. Salami and sopressata are similar so, you may want to have only one or the other. Imported prosciutto, especially Parma prosciutto, is superior to domestic varieties. Capocollo comes hot and mild – hot will keep longer. If you have a choice, pick mortadella without pistachio. Have at least one cheese sliced, like provolone, for those like my Dad, who will undoubtedly want to make sandwiches. As for the parmesan, try Parmigiano Reggiano. Once the crunchy morsels of this delectable cheese hit your palate you are almost certain to never be satisfied with any other type of Parmigiano. Following are some suggestions but let your likings and imagination be your guide.

Meats and Fish	*Cheese*	*Vegetables*
• sopressata	• fontina	• a variety of olives
• salami	• gorgonzola	• marinated artichoke hearts
• capocollo	• mozzarella	• marinated mushrooms
• prosciutto	• provolone	• pickles
• mortadella	• parmesan	• roasted peppers
• pepperoni	• munster	• pepperocini
• anchovies		• garbanzo or fava beans
• sardines		

Arrange attractively on platters and in bowls. Serve with baskets of good Italian bread and/or crunchy breadsticks. Wash down with plenty of wine or as my Aunt Teresa used to do – wine mixed with her favorite sparkling soda.

Fritters

These small savory or sweet cakes with their slightly crisp exteriors and fluffy, steamy centers are best when freshly cooked and served piping hot. Although there are many types of fritters, all are made by binding their ingredients with a pancake-like batter and frying in hot oil. There should be only enough batter to hold all the ingredients together as the fritters should showcase their filling and not be too cakey.

Our family made fritters (or grispelle as they are called in Calebrese) with vegetables, fruits, potatoes or rice. But, in Calabria, my mom's family also made fritters, with small fish called rosa marina because they were only the size of a rosemary leaf. In actuality, they were immature, or neonata, sardines and anchovies. The fish were washed and used whole to make fritters - my mom says these were absolutely delicious and her favorite grispelle. Instead of meat, fritters of all varieties were cooked and eaten often.

Zucchini fritters were most commonly made in our family although we some-time made them with cooked rice. My Nonna Zilioli also made sweet, apple fritters which are more like a breakfast treat, dessert or yummy snack.

½ c. all-purpose flour
¼ tsp. baking powder
¼ c. milk
2 eggs
2 c. shredded zucchini
½ c. grated parmesan cheese
¼ c. chopped fresh parsley
1 clove garlic mashed
½ tsp. each salt and pepper
1-1½ c. oil for frying

Shred the zucchini on a box grater. In a large mixing bowl, mix together the flour, baking powder, milk and eggs just until the batter comes together - be careful to not over mix. Add the zucchini, cheese, parsley, garlic, and salt and pepper and mix thoroughly.

Heat the oil in a sauté pan until hot but not smoky, about 325°. (If the oil is too hot, the fritters will brown on the outside and the centers will not be cooked through). Carefully drop heaping tablespoons of the fritter batter into the hot oil leaving about 1" between fritters. Cook for about 2-3 minute or until nicely browned then turn and cook the other side for another couple of minutes. Drain on paper towels and salt immediately. Serve while still hot.

Makes about a dozen

VARIATIONS: Substitute cut zucchini flowers, cooked mashed potatoes, or cooked rice for the shredded zucchini.

Antipasto alla NonnaZ

My Nonna Zilioli made this zesty antipasto that my Nonno liked as a condiment on sandwiches. It is also a delicious appetizer served with crackers or as a topping for crostini. Because it is somewhat of a chunky relish, the ingredients need to be cut into recognizable pieces.

1 c. red wine vinegar
¼ c. olive oil
6 oz. can tomato paste
4 stalks diced celery
½ lb. green beans, cleaned and cut into ½" pieces
1 small head cauliflower broken into small florets
1 c. small button mushrooms, cleaned
12 oz. albacore tuna or sardines
1 jar pickled pearl onions
4 oz. green olives with pimentos
2 oz. pitted kalamata olives
salt and pepper

Mix the vinegar, olive oil and tomato paste in a non-reactive dutch oven and bring to a simmer. Add the celery and beans, cover and cook for several minutes.   Add the cauliflower and mushrooms and continue cooking until the vegetables are al dente. Remove from heat, drain the tuna or sardines, pearl onions and olives then mix with the cooked vegetables. Salt and pepper to taste. Cool slightly and store in jars in the refrigerator. Serve chilled.

Bagna Calda

The garlic and anchovies on which Bagna Calda is based, gives this dish its robust flavor and intoxicating aroma. The butter smoothes out the flavor and holds it all together. It is eaten in the fashion that a hungry peasant would eat fondue – without the fancy forks and with lots of bread. As your guests share the steamy, lusciousness of the Bagna Calda they will find themselves sharing stories and engaging in good natured banter as well. That annoying cousin, sister or friend who insists on warning everyone about their cholesterol can and should politely be ignored. Be prepared to describe how this unique dish is made because nearly everyone eating it for the first time will want to know the details.

Bagna Calda is typical of the Piedmontese area of Italy but was introduced to my Dad's family after they immigrated to America by their Bolognese friends at "the hall". My Nonno was involved with a socio-political group of fellow Italian anarchists who periodically held events characterized by big dinners, live music, dancing and general partying. Wine and mixed drinks flowing from the bar and a pinochle game or two accompanied the festivities. I am sure there was much pontification and arguments that ensued but all was in the spirit of fun and fellowship while leisurely eradicating the obvious contradiction of remaining an anarchist while benefiting from capitalism in America. The venue for these gatherings was a rented hall on Gratiot Avenue on the east side of Detroit. Over the years the location of the event became synonymous with the event and partiers themselves. Hence when we speak of "the hall" it's understood that we're referring holistically to the organization, its members, the venue, and the party.

A small hot plate or small sterno chafing dish is necessary to keep the Bagna Calda (which means "hot bath") nice and warm. To balance its richness, Bagna Calda is served with an array of fresh, crispy vegetables. Some favorites are celery, napa cabbage leaves, bok choy, radishes, green onions, bell pepper, cauliflower, mushrooms, carrots and zucchini.

> 8 gloves garlic, peeled
> ¼ c. olive oil
> 3 cans anchovies, packed in olive oil
> 1½ sticks unsalted butter
> cut fresh vegetables for dipping

In a small frying pan on low heat, slowly cook the garlic in the olive oil until the garlic gloves are soft and buttery but not browned in any way. Mash the garlic with the back of a fork and add the anchovies along with the packing oil – buy anchovies in olive oil whenever possible. Mash the anchovies and continue cooking and stirring until the Bagna Calda is a smooth sauce. Off heat, add one stick of butter cut into pieces, and stir until the butter is melted.

Place the Bagna Calda in a small chafing dish or in a pan that will fit on the hot plate. Serve with the fresh vegetables and lots of crusty Italian bread. Use the vegetables to dip and scoop the Bagna Calda and the bread to catch the drippings. Don't be afraid to dip the bread directly into the Bagna Calda. To appear a bit less indulgent, you can employ this trick – scoop a lot, then let it drip. As the Bagna Calda is eaten, add portions of the remaining ½ stick butter as needed to maintain its consistency. Glasses of wine provide the perfect finish. Hope for leftovers because Bagna Calda over pasta is fantastic.

Serves 6-8

Olives

For millennium olives have been the life-blood of the Mediterranean region so it is no surprise that they often appeared at many of our meals. My mom's family owned farming land on the Mediterranean Ocean which of course included olive trees. They employed a variety of preserving methods making olives readily available year around. Brining, salting and marinating olives, often with herbs and peppers, were common practices.

My Nonna Crocco often marinated olives in a 3-4 gallon earthen crock that she kept in her basement. The crock was capped with a wooden lid that loosely fit the inner dimension of the crock's opening. The lid had about a 1" hole in the center and Nonna weighed it down with a small, bowling ball sized rock. Whenever Nona wanted olives, she would merely go to the crock and retrieve a bowlful.

When it was time to replenish the olive crock, my mom, sister and I sometimes helped. Several days prior, Nonna blanched the olives and then soaked them in cold water for 3-4 days changing the water several times a day. We helped with the pitting and preserving. Nonna lined us up on her work counter downstairs where we pitted the olives by lightly smashing them between two bricks. Nonna layered 3-4" of pitted olives with cloves of fresh garlic, oregano, hot peppers and salt. When the crock was full, she covered it with the wooden lid and rock. In a few weeks she had marinated olives. Thinking back, I'm not sure where she got the rock, but she was very resourceful and if Nonna needed a rock she evidently managed to find one.

Today, many grocery and speciality stores offer "olive bars" containing all varieties of olives prepared in many different ways so there is really no need to preserve one's own olives. However, one should still enjoy then often.

> 1 c. each of several olive varieties
> bag of bread sticks

Place the olives in bowls and serve with bread sticks. These are a great accompaniment to wine and cocktails.

Stuffed Mushrooms

My Aunt Louise (mom's younger sister), married a hard-working, young Italian immigrant (Uncle Lino) who during his career built a large and successful mushroom producing and processing business. So of course, whenever we visited Aunt Louise, mushrooms were sure to grace her beautiful family dinners. I remember one such dinner where she first introduced us to stuffed mushrooms, which at the time, I thought were so exotic and elegant. Eating them was such an exciting, new culinary experience and they were oh so scrumptious!

I often make stuffed mushrooms when I want to serve an appetizer that's just a little bit fancy. They look pretty when artfully arranged on a platter and like Aunt Louise's, I find they vanish quickly.

24-28 2" diameter mushrooms
½ onion, diced small
2 stalks celery, diced small
10 mushroom stems, chopped small
2 Tbl. olive oil
3 hot Italian sausage
4-5 c. fresh breadcrumbs
⅓ c. chopped fresh parsley
1½ tsp. thyme
½ c. grated Parmesan cheese
1 egg
1 c. chicken broth
salt and pepper to taste

Wash and drain the mushrooms. Pull the stems out and with the tip of a tea-spoon scrape out the remaining stem and underside of the mushroom to form a little "cup" that will hold the stuffing. Be careful to not break the sides of the mushroom while you are scraping them out. If you cup the palm of you hand and hold the mushroom there so that you are supporting the sides of the mushroom as you scrape around the inside, it will help to keep the mushroom intact

To make the stuffing, sauté the onions, celery and mushroom stems in the olive oil – salt and pepper while cooking. When soft, about 7 minutes, place in a mixing bowl. Remove the casing from the Italian sausage and brown lightly. Break-up the sausage as it cooks so it is more-or-less the consistency of cooked ground beef. Drain the fat and add the sausage to the bowl with the onions, celery. and mushroom stems Add the fresh breadcrumbs, parsley, thyme, Parmesan cheese and some salt and pepper - mix well. Slightly beat the egg and mix with the chicken broth. Slowly pour the egg and broth mixture over the stuffing and mix to moisten. (You might need to add a little more or less broth).

Oil a shallow baking dish that is large enough to hold the mushroom caps. Lightly salt and pepper the inside of the caps. Using a teaspoon, mound and firmly pack the stuffing into each cap and place in the baking dish. Bake in a 400° oven for about 20-25 minutes or until browned.

NOTE: To make fresh breadcrumbs, use good quality, sliced white or Italian bread and run it through a food processor.

Salads

About Salads

There are many types of salads and cold dishes containing either cooked or raw crisp vegetables. Several of my favorites and the most commonly served by my family are included in this section on salads. Although all of them are traditional, tasty salads, the fresh, green salad is by far the staple salad at the Italian dinner table. I can scarcely remember a dinner that did not include a green salad of

some sort. Unlike Americans, Italians eat their salad last however, our family does not usually have formal dinners served in courses. Instead, the salad is served in a large bowl placed on the table together with the entrees and side-dishes. Some of the most memorable salads are the simple, leaf-lettuce salads made from freshly picked lettuce straight from the garden, dressed lightly with oil and vinegar. These simple salads stress the point that a good green salad must start with tasty, crisp greens and should never be heavily coated with dressing which can mask the delectable flavor of the fresh vegetables.

To prepare greens for salad select several varieties which may include romaine, leaf, red-leaf, escarole, endive, radicchio and iceberg. To clean the lettuce, remove and discard all the outer large leaves. Do not use any bruised or tough portions. With romaine lettuce, also remove the very top portion of the leaves if they seem over developed and tough. Do not cut the leaves away from the stem, instead leave the heads intact. Wash the heads under running, cold water while gently separating the leaves so the water can run between them, shake out any excess water, then drain upside-down for about five minutes in a colander or drain board. Lay the lettuce heads on clean tea towels and wrap the towels tightly around the lettuce. If you are using loose greens for example, spinach or arugula, wash and drain as above, lay on a tea towel more or less in a single layer, then roll up the towel like a jelly roll. Place the towels with the lettuce in a plastic grocery bag and refrigerate for at least several hours. Greens may be stored in the rolls for 2-3 days.

Escarole Salad

Escarole is typically served as a cooked green usually with cannellini or other white beans. However, the tender inner leaves are surprisingly a robust, tasty salad green with a slightly bitter but not unpleasant flavor. Shaved parmesan cheese is a nice addition to this salad although our family served it simply dressed.

> 1 head of escarole
> ¼ c. olive oil
> 2-4 Tbls. red wine vinegar
> salt and pepper

Remove the large, outer leaves of the escarole then wash and dry the inner, light colored heart. Cut away the stem then slice the heart of the escarole crosswise into about ½" strips. Place into a large bowl, dress with the olive oil, vinegar, salt and pepper and serve immediately. If desired, shave good quality parmesan cheese on each serving.

NOTE: Save the outer leaves and cook for a vegetable side dish.

Cicoria Salad

Cicoria is the Italian word for chicory, but we used it to refer to any type of wild green. In Italy, wild greens were common additions to a typical diet. They were picked during early spring while still tender and made into a fresh green salad. During WWII my mom's family was unable to safely work on their farming properties so wild greens were pretty much the only fresh greens they ate. Because wild greens are somewhat more bitter than cultivated greens, they are only suitable for green salad when very young and tender. Once they begin to mature, they must first be cooked and are equally delicious.

During my childhood, the women of our family continued with the tradition of picking wild greens in the spring. My mom, Aunt Teresa and Nonna Zilioli knew of several undeveloped lots and parks in the vicinity that provided an abundance of cicoria. In early spring we would all pile into the car and head off to go cicoria picking. The adults, each armed with a brown grocery bag and small knife, would walk slowly, bent over, combing the fields for sprouting cicoria. We kids would help, but mostly we just played and had fun. I remember one such outing when a couple of boys seeing us bent over digging in the grass with our bags and knives yelled out from across the street, "Hey lady, whatcha doing?" My sister, Gina, stood up and exasperatedly replied, "picking cicoria, what does it look like?"

With the availability of a wide variety of salad greens, there is really no need to go cicoria picking. Substitute arugula or other 'wilder' cultivated greens for a green salad and use dandelion greens or swiss chard for the cooked cicoria salad.

> 5 c. fresh cicoria
> 1 clove fresh garlic
> ¼ c. olive oil
> 2-4 Tbls. red wine vinegar
> salt and pepper to taste

Clean, wash, drain and dry the cicoria. If they are mature, steam for about 5-10 minutes or until tender, drain and chill. Press or finely chop the garlic and mix with the olive oil and vinegar. Pour the dressing over the cicoria and toss with salt and pepper. Serve immediately with plenty of Italian bread.

Green Salad

The key to a great green salad is in the freshness and quality of the greens and is best if made from a variety of greens. When selecting greens, keep in mind the flavor, texture and appearance that each will contribute to the salad. Romaine, Boston, spinach, green leaf and red leaf tend to have the most flavor. Romaine, spinach and green leaf have more texture and hold up to heavier dressings. Boston and red leaf add tenderness. Some of the curly leaf lettuces like endive, escarole and arugula are somewhat bitter but used sparingly add robustness and a nice visual touch. Iceberg lettuce has very little flavor but is a good texture enhancer since it is one of the crunchiest. The dark red pigments in radicchio will add color. Add to the greens whatever other vegetables you like. For a heartier salad include hard boiled eggs, cheeses and/or cold meats like grilled chicken, salami, ham or tuna.

Here is one of my favorite green salads:

> 8 cups of salad greens
> 1 red bell pepper
> 1 cucumber
> 1 small red onion
> 5 radishes
> 1 medium tomato or 1 c. cherry tomatoes
> 1 can garbanzo beans
> dressing and salt and pepper to taste

Break or cut the greens into bite size pieces and place in a large salad bowl omitting any large stems or bruised portions. Slice and add the bell pepper, cucumber, onion and radishes and lightly mix together. Drain the garbanzos in a strainer and rinse with cold water. Lay them on a towel and rub lightly to dry off the water then sprinkle over the top of the salad. Cut the tomato into pieces or cut cherry tomatoes in half and lay on top the garbanzos. Dress immediately prior to serving.

Marinated Vegetable Salad

This salad can be made with one of several different vegetables. Each has its own unique twist but is made basically the same way. Marinated vegetable salads are an excellent accompaniment to a summer dinner or lunch. Because there is no mayonnaise in the dressing they are particularly well suited for picnics and cookouts.

Four different vegetables that are commonly used for this salad are potatoes, green beans, mushrooms and cauliflower. Try each one.

8 c. potatoes, green beans, mushrooms or cauliflower
2-3 large gloves garlic
1 c. fresh parsley, chopped
⅓ c. olive oil
¼ c. red wine vinegar
salt and pepper to taste

Clean and wash the vegetables, if using cauliflower break into 1½" florets. Steam the vegetables until tender but still al dente. If using potatoes, boil them until they can be pierced with a fork but are not so soft that they fall apart. When the potatoes are cool enough to handle cut into bite-size pieces. While vegetables are still warm, mix well with the garlic, parsley and olive oil. Add the vinegar, salt and pepper and mix again. Cover and chill thoroughly. Mix before serving.

Makes 8-10 servings

Tomato and Onion Salad

When there is an abundance of fresh, ripe tomatoes from the garden this salad is a delicious summer side dish. Because of the mild acidity of the tomatoes, this salad needs no vinegar.

> 5-6 medium ripe tomatoes
> 1 small red onion or sweet white onion
> 3 Tbls. olive oil
> 1 Tbl. oregano
> salt and pepper to taste

Cut the tomatoes into bite-size pieces and place in a bowl. Cut the onion in half and slice thinly. Add onion to the tomatoes along with the olive oil, oregano and salt and pepper. Mix well.

Fresh Radish Salad

One of the first vegetables harvested from the backyard garden are radishes and their presence at the dinner table is a sure sign that the bounty of the summer garden is just around the corner. Garden radishes have a characteristic spicy crunch but are never hot because they ripen while the summer temperatures are still cool. When we were kids we considered this salad a special treat not only for its fresh, delicate flavor but also because it was fun to eat. Radish salad is especially good with plenty of home baked bread.

15-20 fresh radishes
½ c. olive oil
2 Tbl. salt

Clean the radishes leaving about 1-2" of greens on each radish. Trim off the root and cut an X about two-thirds of the way into the end of the radish. Put the oil and salt into a small cup and place in the center of a plate. Arrange the radishes around the cup with the green tops facing outwards. Using the radish green as a 'handle', swirl the radish in the oil and salt and eat the root portion discarding the 'handle'.

Roasted Bell Peppers

Roasting the peppers accentuates their flavor and intensifies the sweetness of their sugar. Peppers are most easily roasted on a grill but can also be roasted on an open fire or under the broiler of your oven.

We made roasted peppers on the gas burners of Nonna Crocco's basement stove. She would turn on a couple burners, place 2-3 peppers on each and turn them until they were charred and blistered on all sides.

> 6 bell peppers, any color or combination
> 1 medium clove garlic
> 2 Tbls. olive oil
> salt and pepper to taste

Place whole bell peppers on a medium hot grill. Turn the peppers periodically so that their skins are entirely browned and blistered, about 3-4 minutes on

each side. Be careful not to let them get too dark or burned. The idea is to blister the skins sufficiently so they peel off easily, but to not get them so dark that the pepper's flesh underneath chars and sticks to the skins whereby making them difficult to peel. Place the roasted peppers in a paper bag or in a large bowl until they are cool enough to handle. Using a small knife, peel the blistered skin from the peppers, remove the seeds and membrane and cut the peppers into 1" strips.

Place the roasted pepper strips in a bowl. Crush the garlic with a garlic press and add to the peppers along with the olive oil and salt and pepper. Mix well and chill.

Serves 8-10

Dressing

Jennie's Creamy Italian Dressing

This is my mom's creation that takes advantage of packaged salad dressing seasoning. She makes about a quart at a time and keeps it refrigerated in an easy pour bottle. It is a guaranteed crowd pleaser.

> 2 packages Good Season Italian salad dressing mix
> 4-5 cloves fresh garlic, peeled and crushed
> 2 c. olive oil
> 1 c. red wine vinegar
> ¼ c. water

Place the Good Season's, garlic, vinegar and water in a blender. With the blender on high, slowly pour in the oil in a slow steady stream. The blending action emulsifies the oil resulting in a smooth, creamy texture. Transfer the dressing to a bottle and keep refrigerated. Shake well before using.

NOTE: 1/3 c. of the red wine vinegar can be replaced with balsamic vinegar.

Oil and Vinegar

The delicate tastes and delightful textures of a truly good salad need no more dressing than a hint of quality olive oil and a splash of vinegar. Of course, red wine vinegar is the classic vinegar accompaniment for Italian salads however, a mixture of red wine vinegar and fresh lemon juice or balsamic vinegar are equally good.

When dressing a salad, always add the oil first and toss slightly before adding the vinegar or salt. The oil will protect the greens from the wilting effect of vinegar and salt and will keep the salad nice and crisp. I find that sea salt and fresh ground pepper add the perfect finish.

> 1 serving green salad
> 1-2 Tbls. good quality olive oil
> 1-2 Tbls. red wine vinegar
> sea salt and fresh ground pepper to taste

Drizzle the olive oil over the salad and toss. Add the vinegar and salt and toss until the salad is well dressed. Top with fresh ground pepper. Serve and enjoy immediately.

Vinaigrette

The addition of lemon juice makes this dressing a little more mellow than a traditional oil and vinegar dressing. This dressing is best if made at least several hours ahead of time so the flavors have a chance to blend. Since olive oil has a tendency to become very viscous when refrigerated, this dressing should be left at room temperature for 5-10 minutes prior to dressing the salad.

1 large clove fresh garlic
1 tsp. salt
1 c. olive oil
⅓ c. red wine vinegar
1 fresh lemon, juiced
1 Tbl. dried oregano or basil

Crush the garlic and place in the bottom of a small jar along with the salt. Using the back of a spoon, mash the garlic and salt together. Add the oil, vinegar, lemon juice and oregano or basil. Place the lid on the jar, shake vigorously and refrigerate for at least several hours. Remove the dressing from the refrigerator about ten minutes before dressing the salad. Shake well before using.

Soups

Mother's Chicken Brodo

To make a really good soup, one must use a really good broth. When my mom and dad's generation were living in Italy, soups often lacked tastiness because the meats needed to make broth were often not available. Instead, most soup stocks were made by flavoring hot water with lard and salt if one was in southern Italy, and flavoring with butter and salt if in northern Italy.

As kids, we always called broth or stock, brodo and although I now almost never use the word (most people would have no idea what I was talking about) the word brodo still conjures up homey, comforting memories. Brodo is easy to make and can serve as the basis for soups as varied as your imagination.

When I was in my twenties and still learning to run my own household, I often bought chicken because is seemed so economical. However, by the time I re-moved the skin, set aside the back, neck and wing tips and trimmed off the excess fat, I often questioned just how economical this bird really was. I de-veloped a greater appreciation for the true economy of chicken during one of my mom and dad's visits to Dillard, Oregon, where my mom showed me how she made brodo with what I had considered 'unusable' chicken parts. And to think, I had been throwing away these parts for years and buying canned broth for making soups!

Since then, I save in the freezer, the backs, necks and wing tips from several chickens and use them to make brodo. Sometimes, of course, I use an entire chicken. The brodo, once made, can be stored in the freezer and the meat salvaged from the bones can be added to the soup.

> 1 medium chicken, or parts from 3-4 chickens
> 3-4 ribs celery
> 1 large onion
> 1 c. parsley leaves
> 3-4 bay leaves
> 2 Tbls. black pepper corns
> 1 gallon water, approximately
> 2 Tbl. salt or to taste

Place the chicken in a large stock pot. Add enough water to cover the chicken by about an inch. Wash and clean the celery and cut into large pieces 3-4 inches long. Peel the onion and cut it into 4 wedges. Add the celery, onion, parsley, bay leaves, pepper corns and salt to the chicken and water. Cover the pot and heat on medium-high until boiling. Reduce the heat and simmer for about 1½ hours stirring occasionally. Skim off any foam that might collect at the surface of the simmering brodo.

Cool slightly, adjust salt and strain through a colander into another large pot. If the brodo is not going to be used immediately, refrigerate the brodo or transfer it to smaller containers and freeze. Once chilled, the chicken fat will solidify in a layer on top of the brodo. This will help preserve the brodo and can be easily removed and discarded before the brodo is used.

When the chicken or bones are cool enough to handle, remove the meat from the bones and use in soup, salad, pâté or anything else you can think of.

Makes about 1 gallon

Chicken Soup

Several blocks from my Nonna and Nonno Crocco's house in Detroit was a small chicken processing plant. Chickinaro is the only thing I ever heard it called and I am still not sure if Chickinaro is the name of the business or its proprietor. As children, we sometimes spent the night at Nonna's and I distinctly remember my sister and I walking there with Nonna to buy chicken and eggs. Since a supply of fresh chicken was so convenient, my Nonna made chicken soup for lunch nearly every Saturday during the first several years following her and her family's move from Italy.

Nonna would buy a large chicken from Chickinaro who often gave Nonna an extra package of chicken feet to add to her soup. Nonna saved the breast and thighs for other dishes and used the back, legs, wings and feet for her soup. She also added vegetables, which were served to each person along with a piece of cooked chicken.

This is a delicious and satisfying soup (even without the chicken feet) and still makes a great Saturday lunch.

> 1 large chicken
> 6 medium potatoes
> 10 carrots
> 6 stalks celery
> 1 large onion
> 1 c. fresh parsley
> 1 bay leaf
> 2 Tbls. salt
> 1 tsp. black pepper

Clean the chicken and cut it into serving size pieces. Peel and wash the celery.then cut into thirds. Peel the onion and cut into 6-8 large pieces. Place the cut-up chicken, celery and onion into a stockpot along with the parsley, bay leaf salt and pepper. Add fresh cold water to just cover the ingredients and bring to a boil, then reduce the heat so the soup is simmering and cook for 40 minutes stirring occasionally.

In the meantime, peel the potatoes and carrots leaving the potatoes whole and cutting the carrots crosswise into thirds. Add to the pot, let the soup come back to a simmer (raise the heat a bit if needed) and simmer for 20-25 minutes more or until the potatoes and carrots are fork tender.

For each serving, place in a large soup bowl, a piece of chicken, one potato, several pieces of carrot and celery and several ladles of broth. Serve piping hot with fresh bread.

Makes 6 servings

Minestra Col Lach

Minestra col lach is a typical northern Italy dish. The abundance of milk products in the region form the basis of this soup which, was commonly made during the summer when warm temperatures made it difficult to store and preserve milk. It is a no frills soup that, except for the lack of vegetables, is not totally unlike American cream and chowder soups. My Nonna Zilioli made this soup and although she did not serve this soup at our family dinners, she did make it often to stretch the family food budget while she was raising my dad, Aunt Teresa and Uncle Jack. Aunt Teresa said that they liked this soup because Nonna's other soups consisted of pasta cooked in a broth of water and butter and, minestra col lach, in comparison, was a tasty alternative.

Nonna made three variations of this soup: riso col lach (rice), pasta col lach (noodles) and polenta col lach (polenta). Basically, the soup consists of either rice, pasta or polenta cooked in thickened milk. My Uncle Jack, who owned and operated a pattern making shop, told my Nonna that he often got an urge for this soup while he was working. Remembering Uncle Jack's comments, my dad, when working with his shop-smith, realized that the smell of singed wood as it passed through an electric saw blade was reminiscent of the smell of hot, boiling milk that accompanied Nonna's minestra col lach. Dad and Uncle Jack later confirmed this association since Uncle Jack only got the urge when he was working with his saws. It just goes to show how much our memories of home, childhood and food are all wrapped up together.

	4 c. whole milk
	2 c. rice
OR	2 c. thin homemade noodles
OR	2 c. cooked polenta cut into ½" cubes tossed in flour
	salt to taste

Place the milk in a heavy pot and bring to a slow boil. Slowly add the rice, noodles or polenta to the milk while stirring gently. Add salt and stir occasionally. If making polenta col lach, cook until the milk is thickened and the polenta is heated through. If making riso or pasta col lach, cook until rice or pasta is cooked. Serve piping hot.

Serves 4-6

Pasta e Fagioli

Pasta combined with legumes is a common theme in Italian cuisine. With the abundance of pasta shapes and sizes, and the many varieties of legumes, the number of pasta e fagioli dishes is endless. I would guess that there is at least one variation of this dish for each cook that has ever prepared it.

My mom's version of pasta e fagioli is a tomato based soup, that is both hearty and tasty. In Italy, this soup was made with water in which lard was added for flavor. However, Mom omits the lard and flavors the soup with chicken broth instead.

1 lb. dried Northern White beans
2 Tbls. olive oil
2 slices pancetta or bacon, well chopped (optional)
1 large onion
8 cloves garlic
½ c. tomato paste
6-7 c. chicken broth
1 Tbl. oregano
1 tsp. thyme
2 tsp. crushed red pepper (optional)
7 oz. ditali or tubetti pasta, uncooked (4 c. cooked)
½ c. pecorino or parmesan cheese
salt and pepper to taste

Soak the beans either overnight or for 3-4 hours in fresh water. Discard soaking water. Put the beans into a heavy pot with enough fresh water to cover by about 1 inch. Add a couple teaspoons of salt and 5 of the garlic cloves, cover the pot and simmer the beans, stirring occasionally, for about 1½ hours or until they are tender. Drain the beans if there is excess water remaining after cooking.

In a heavy pot, cook the pancetta/bacon with the olive oil until it begins to render and is slightly browned. Chop the onion and remaining 3 cloves of garlic and add to the pot. If you want the pasta e fagioli a little spicy, also add the red pepper. Sauté until the onions are tender, about 5-7 minutes. Add the cooked beans and stir. Put the tomato paste into a small bowl and mix with a small amount of the broth so that the tomato paste is liquidity. Pour the tomato paste and remaining broth into the pot with the beans. Add the oregano and thyme, and season with salt and pepper. Bring the beans to a simmer and continue cooking uncovered for about 20 minutes. While the beans are simmering, cook the pasta separately until not quite done. Drain well and add to the beans. Let the pasta e fagioli cook for a few more minutes. When serving, pass the cheese - pecorino is most authentic but parmesan more available.

NOTE: For a quicker soup, you can use four 15 ounce cans of Northern White beans drained of the liquid instead of cooking dried beans yourself.

Makes 8-10 servings

Minestrone Soup

Minestrone soup is probably one of the most classic of Italian soups. And although most people probably associate this soup with waiters singing 'O Sole Mio' and checkered table cloths, I always associate this soup with my Nonna Zilioli. She generally made minestrone soup when she wanted to use the leftovers she had in the refrigerator. Because Nonna's resourcefulness was so apparent when she made minestrone, as kids we called it "Everything but the Kitchen Sink Soup". Nonna nearly always had a piece of roast, pork or sausage to add to the soup. The vegetables and their quantities varied somewhat by what was on hand or in season. Zucchini, legumes, greens and pasta were nearly always included.

Typically, minestrone soup has a tomato based broth however, instead of tomatoes my Nonna Crocco often used split peas. The result is a thicker more hearty soup. Either way, served with fresh Italian bread, minestrone soup is a delicious and satisfying meal in itself.

2 c. cooked roast or Italian sausage chopped
1 medium onion
3 Tbl olive oil
3 cloves fresh garlic finely chopped
3 stalks celery
5 carrots
3 medium potato
2 medium zucchini
2 c. fresh green beans
1 can garbanzo beans
1 c. cooked spinach or other greens, chopped
1 c. spaghetti broken into 1 inch pieces or other pasta
1 Tbl. oregano
2 Tbl. basil
1 tsp. thyme
½ c. chopped fresh parsley
12 c. chicken broth
1 28 oz. can stewed tomatoes chopped

OR   1 c. split peas
½ c. grated parmesan cheese
salt and pepper to taste

Dice the onion, slice the celery and carrots, and sauté in a large soup pot along with the garlic and olive oil. Peel and dice the potatoes and add to the pot. Add the broth, tomatoes, oregano, basil and thyme, and bring to a simmer. String and clean the green beans and cut into ½ inch pieces. Dice the zucchini. Add the green beans and zucchini to the soup and cook the vegetables about 15 minutes. Add the spinach, garbanzos, meat and split peas if using. Adjust the seasoning and salt and pepper to taste. Simmer the soup for about 40 minutes stirring occasionally.

In a separate pot, cook the pasta until not quite done. Drain the pasta and add to the soup along with the parsley. Continue cooking the soup for a couple minutes just until the pasta is done. Serve with the parmesan cheese, black pepper and plenty of Italian bread.

Makes 12 servings

Pane Cotto

Variations of this soup, consisting of bread soaked with hot broth, can be found throughout Italy. Pane cotto, literally cooked bread, was often eaten for lunch or given to people when they were sick. Since bread was commonly preserved by drying or toasting until hard, pane cotto was a method used to reconstitute the bread while adding flavor and warmth with hot broth. An extravagant variation includes a beaten egg in the hot broth. Be sure to use a hearty bread that will retain its texture once it is soaked with broth.

4 c. hot broth
8 slices dried Italian bread
½ c. grated parmesan cheese
freshly grated black pepper to taste

Slice a loaf of good quality Italian bread and lay the slices on a cookie sheet. Place in a 350° oven for about 20 minutes or until the bread is dry and crispy. While the bread is crisping, heat the broth to a slow boil. When the bread is crisp and slightly browned, remove from the oven and place two slices of bread in each of four bowls. Pour one cup of broth in each bowl so that the bread is soaked with broth. Sprinkle with cheese and black pepper and serve immediately.

Makes 4 servings

Ricotta Ball Soup

This soup begins with a ricotta mixture similar to that used for ravioli or mani-cotti filling. It is a light, tasty soup that makes a wonderful lunch or quick dinner. My mom did not make Ricotta Ball soup as often as she made other soups so it was always a special treat for us. The whimsical, little cheese balls bathing in hot, steamy broth are both delightful and delicious.

1 lb. ricotta cheese
1 large clove garlic, pressed
¾ c. bread crumbs
½ c. fresh parsley chopped
½ c. grated parmesan cheese
2 tsp. oregano
½ tsp. black pepper
½ tsp. salt
2 eggs
8 c. chicken broth

Mix together (but don't beat) all ingredients except for the chicken broth. Heat the broth in a wide pot until it comes to a slow boil. Using about ⅓ cup of the ricotta mixture at a time, shape into a ball and carefully place each ball into the boiling broth. Maintain a slow boil and cook for about 20 minutes stirring very carefully once or twice. Remove from heat and cool until boiling has stopped. Place a couple of ricotta balls in each bowl and ladle some of the chicken broth over them. Serve immediately.

Makes about 9 ricotta balls

Pure and Simple Soup

The beginning to an Italian meal is often a bowl of warm, uncomplicated soup. These soups consist of homemade chicken broth in which rice, pastina or fresh pasta noodles are cooked. Sometimes, bits of cut up chicken used to make the broth are also included. The soup is served piping hot and topped with fresh grated parmesan cheese.

Rice soup was always my dad's favorite. The rice is only parboiled in water and cooked the rest of the way in the broth so that the rice kernels puff-up and soften as they become filled with chicken broth. The result is a delicate, yet tasty soup. We kids liked pastina soup. Not only because of its appealing mild flavor but also because it was fun to eat. We thought it was really amazing that the tiny pasta balls could be swallowed without chewing. I am not sure why we got such a kick out of this, except that we were kids; need I say more. Pasta leftover from making ravioli was generally cut into thin noodles for fresh pasta noodle soup. It is a delicious classic. Whichever variety of pure and simple soup served, it is sure to be the perfect beginning to an enjoyable meal.

8 c. chicken broth
1 c. parboiled rice, pastina or fresh pasta noodles
1 c. cut up boiled chicken (optional)
½ c. fresh grated parmesan cheese

Place the broth in a large pot and bring to a medium boil. Add the parboiled rice, pastina or noodles and cook about 10 minutes or until done. (The rice will take a little longer.) If using cooked chicken, add and heat through. Serve hot and pass the parmesan cheese.

Makes 6-8 servings

Tortellini

This is by far the most delicious soup ever made. These tiny filled pastas, cooked and served in hot, steamy broth are a true culinary delight. Tortellini, in my mind, is almost synonymous with dinner at Aunt Teresa's. We could always count on her serving this soup as a first course for any family dinner she hosted. This soup is so delicious, that there was always the temptation to have seconds. However, the real challenge was to resist, because if you didn't, you would have no room for whatever scrumptious main course Aunt Teresa was serving.

Tortellini was brought into our family by Uncle Al. It is a traditional Bolognese dish that Aunt Teresa learned to make from her mother-in-law, Maria Fabbri. I never had dinner at Nonna Maria's (that's what Laura and David called her so we did too) but, Laura told me about going to Nonna Maria's and finding the women gathered in the kitchen stuffing small squares of pasta for the dinner's tortellini soup.

Since each tortellini must be made individually by hand, and Aunt Teresa worked as a school teacher, she would spend many evening before the dinner fashioning these delectable little morsels. She then froze each evening's batch until she had made enough for the upcoming dinner. As a kid, I never realized the work and time she spent on us. However, after preparing many large  dinners myself (and having a few years behind me), I have come to appreciate all that she did, and to recognize the love she poured into these meals.

2 chicken breasts, bone-in with skin
1 chicken thigh, bone-in with skin
2 large pork chops
1 tsp. crushed or ground rosemary
1 tsp. thyme
½ tsp. sage
3 Tbls. butter
¾ c. white wine
2 slices mortadella, cut into small squares
1 c. grated parmesan cheese
¼ tsp. nutmeg
4 c. homemade pasta
10 c. chicken broth
salt and pepper

Rub the chicken breasts and pork chops with the rosemary, thyme and sage. Sprinkle with salt and pepper. Heat the butter in a large heavy skillet and brown the chicken and pork chops, about 4-5 minutes per side. When browned, pour in the white wine, cover and simmer for about 12 minutes, turning occasionally. Remove the meat from the pan and allow to cool.

Remove the meat from the bones reserving the fat from the pork chops, skin from the chicken, and the cooking liquid. Place the meat and cooking liquid in a food processor along with the pork fat, skin and mortadella. Process until very fine in texture. Transfer the ground meat to a bowl along with the parmesan cheese, nutmeg and some salt, if needed. Work the mixture with your hands until it holds together, if the filling seems too dry add an egg or a little water.

With a hand cranked pasta machine or rolling pin, roll the pasta, using ½ c. at a time, into a sheet about ⅛ " thick. Cut the pasta into 1" squares. Fashion the tortellini, one at a time, by placing a small dollop of filling, the size of a garbanzo bean, in the middle of a pasta square. Fold the pasta in half around the

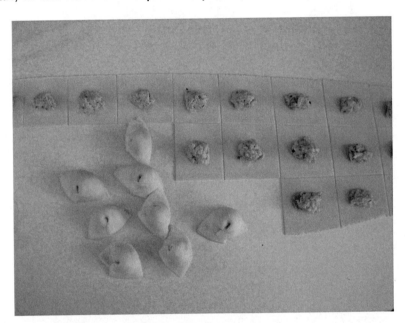

filling pressing the edges to seal. With the folded edge towards you, hold each corner of the folded edge between your thumb and index finger, thumbs on top. Bring the two corners slightly forward and together tucking the pasta under the dollop of filling to form a small 'hat' shape. Press the corners together to seal. Place on cookie sheets and continue until all the pasta and filling are used. To freeze the tortellini, place cookie sheets with a single layer of tortellini in the freezer until the tortellini are frozen. Once frozen, the tortellini can be transferred to and stored in freezer bags.

To make soup, bring the chicken broth to a boil. Drop about four cups (this is enough for approximately 8 servings) of tortellini, a few at a time, into the broth. Cook for about 10-15 minutes or until the pasta is cooked, gently stirring occasionally. Serve immediately with parmesan cheese.

NOTE: Legend has it that tortellini are supposed to resemble Venus' navel so that if you turn one over after you shape it, it should look like a neat round belly button.

You can make tortelloch (aka tortollone - large tortellini) by doubling the size. Tortelloch are typically prepared with browned butter, cream sauce or sugo instead of cooked in broth.

Makes about 400 tortellini

Trippa

My Nonna Zilioli made trippa. It is very similar to minestrone except that for trippa, the pasta is replaced with tripe (cow's stomach). Tripe is not a food that is commonly found in mainstream American cooking (except maybe as an ingredient for hot-dogs) and is difficult to find in most grocery stores. However, in years past, inner organ meats were generally an inexpensive 'cut' of meat and therefore, offered a way to provide meaty flavor and protein to meals while maintaining an austere food budget.

Today, amid health conscientiousness and financial comfort, no one in our family makes trippa anymore. However, I associate this soup so strongly with my Nonna that I felt compelled to include this recipe.

1½ lbs. tripe
1 medium onion
4 Tbls. butter
2 cloves fresh garlic finely chopped
3 stalks celery
5 carrots
3 medium potatoes
2 medium zucchini
2 c. fresh green beans
1 c. cooked spinach or other green chopped
2 tsp. each basil and oregano
1 tsp. thyme
½ c chopped fresh parsley
10-12 c. chicken broth
½ c. dried split peas
salt and pepper to taste

Thoroughly rinse the tripe and boil for about 25 minutes. Drain and rinse with cool water being sure to rinse between the folds in the tripe and removing any fat. Slice the tripe into small pieces about ⅜" wide and 2" long. Sauté the tripe, garlic and butter in a large soup pot until slightly browned. Dice the onion, celery and carrots, add to the pot and sauté until the vegetables are slightly tender. Peel and dice the potatoes and add to the pot along with the broth, oregano, basil and thyme and bring to a simmer. String and clean the green beans and cut into ½" pieces. Dice the zucchini. Add the green beans, zucchini, spinach and parsley. Adjust the seasoning and salt and pepper to taste.

In the mean time, cook the split peas in a separate pan until done, about 1 hour. Simmer the trippa for about an hour stirring occasionally. Add the cooked split peas, stir and cook for 30-minutes more.

Makes 8-10 servings

Pasta

What You Should Know About Pasta

Nearly everyone associates Italian food with spaghetti; a dish consisting of long, rod-shaped pasta tossed in a tomato sauce. Although this certainly describes a classic pasta dish, it is only one of countless pasta shapes flavored with only one of innumerable sauces. Spaghetti is technically the name of the pasta's shape and literally means, "a length of cord or string." Within the class of pasta called spaghetti, there are several variations determined by the size of the die that was used to make the spaghetti. This information is often included on the packaging of most imported pastas. The next time you are buying pasta, notice that next to the pasta name is a manufacture's number that identifies the particular die. For example, you may find "spaghetti no. 5" as opposed to "spaghetti no. 6." One variety will be slightly thicker or thinner than the other. This subtlety may seem insignificant but, to a true pasta connoisseur it can mean the difference between a merely good and absolutely perfect pasta dinner. There are a total of sixteen different sizes of spaghetti with significant differences in diameter being denoted by different names, for example, capellini, fedelini, vermicelli, spaghettini, spaghetti and spaghettoni.

These variations and nuances apply to most other pasta shapes so that pasta can be found in a vast array of shapes and sizes. The pastas my family commonly used are:

- spaghetti - "a length of cord or string"
- fettuccine - "small ribbons"
- mostaccioli - "small mustaches"
- linguine - "small tongues"
- rigatoni - "grooved tubes"
- tubetti - "little tubes"
- rotini - "small wheels"
- pastina - "tiny dough"
- stellini - "baby stars"

Since entire books are dedicated to the discussion of pasta and their various shapes, sizes and names, I will end here except to point out that pasta ain't spaghetti.

When preparing a pasta dish keep in mind, that the quality of the pasta will have a significant effect on the success of the dish. Without a doubt, fresh, homemade pasta is the most delicious and promises the best results. However, most store bought, imported varieties are very good too. Always use a high quality pasta because it is the texture and bite of the pasta along with its ability to carry and enhance the flavor of the sauce that is responsible for a truly gourmet pasta meal.

In addition to pasta quality, cooking method is extremely important. Pasta should always be cooked in plenty of boiling water that is salted just prior to adding the pasta. Some guidelines to follow are 7 quarts of water and 2 tablespoons of salt for every one pound of pasta. Or (one of my favorites), "it is better to use a gallon too much water than a teaspoon not enough". Once the water is at a full boil, add the salt and pasta. Be sure to keep the pasta sufficiently separated while cooking by stirring and lifting with a pasta or wooden fork. The pasta's shape and size will have a large influence on its cooking time as will whether it is fresh or dried. Consequently, you need to test for doneness by periodically tasting the pasta as it cooks. Pasta should be cooked until it is al dente, in other words, firm and chewy but not in anyway hard or tough. When the pasta is cooked, drain it in a colander, turn it out onto a serving dish and immediately toss with the sauce. Or, put the pasta in the same pan with the sauce and combine adding a bit of the pasta cooking water if needed to moisten or loosen the finished dish. Good pasta will absorb the flavor of the sauce and does so best while hot and freshly cooked.

Our family ate many delicious, wonderful meals but my favorites will always be pasta.

Homemade Pasta

Fresh, homemade pasta is undeniably the best there is. If made completely by hand, a fair amount of kneading and rolling is required to produce the necessary smooth, elastic dough. Although this requires a little time and skill, once you master the process, and as long as you have access to a rolling pin and work surface, you will never be without fresh pasta.

My Nonne, in Italy, made pasta nearly every day. To roll the dough, my Nonna Crocco used a maccarunaro; a wooden rolling pin that resembles a four-foot broomstick. A large wooden board, the timpagno, served as the work surface. Nonna rolled the dough into about a three-foot, perfectly round circle and then cut it into whatever length pasta she needed. She obtained this beautiful round of pasta by rolling the dough several times from center to top, then turning the circle of dough not quite one-fourth turn, rolling, turning, rolling, turning and so on. In this way, she controlled the shape, and the large size was made possible by the length of the maccarunaro. To flip the large round over, Nonna loosely rolled the dough around the maccarunaro, lifted it off the timpagno and merely unrolled it to the opposite side.

If you love fresh pasta and this process seems too time consuming for your busy life, do not despair, a variety of pasta-making machines are available that make fresh pasta-making surprisingly convenient. I have a pasta machine that mixes the dough and then extrudes it though a die of my choice. It is so quick and easy that I can literally put a pot of water on to boil, start making the pasta and by the time the water boils, my pasta is made and ready to be cooked. It is wonderful. Since pasta making instructions come with any pasta making machine you may acquire, I will limit my discussion to hand-make pasta.

This is a good basic pasta dough. I highly recommend semolina flour since it produces a delicious and wonderfully textured pasta although in some regions of Italy, a more soft, tender pasta is preferred so all purpose flour is used instead. You may need to add a little more flour or water than what is specified in order to work the dough to just the right consistency; not at all sticky but smooth and pliable.

3½ c. semolina flour
2 large eggs
¾ c. water
¼ tsp. salt
¼ c. all purpose flour for flouring work surface

To make pasta in the classic way, begin by placing the flour in a mound on your work surface. Make a large depression in the center of the mound so it resembles the cone of a volcano. Break the eggs into the cone and add water (and/or any other ingredients). Using your fingers, mix the eggs and water and slowly add the flour to the egg mixture by pulling the flour from the inside of the cone into the center of the "volcano". The idea here is to have a sufficiently firm dough formed before the walls of the cone are no longer thick enough to hold the egg mixture. Otherwise, the egg mixture will spill out of the cone onto the work surface and you will need to work extremely quickly to complete mixing. This is an ingenious method that utilizes the flour as a mixing bowl, which I believe was developed before kitchens were equipped with adequate mixing bowls and utensils. I have made pasta many times using this method however, I now simply use a large mixing bowl and wooden spoon and avoid any risk of my volcano erupting onto my work surface.

Once the dough is formed, knead it until smooth adding additional flour to your hands and/or work surface to prevent sticking. The dough will be considerably more stiff, and harder to knead than bread dough. Form the dough into a ball, cover it with a clean towel and allow it to "rest" for about 30-minutes. Once rested, work about a cup of dough at a time. Roll the dough on a floured work surface with a rolling pin until it is about a foot long. Fold it into thirds and roll again pulling towards the open, not folded edges. Repeat this 4-5 times or until the dough is soft and pliable. Continue rolling the dough into a round until it is of the desired thickness; a little less than 1/16" for fettuccini. Periodically flour and flip the dough so it does not stick to the work surface.

Lightly flour the top of the round. Start at one side of the round and loosely roll it to the other side. Using a sharp knife cut the roll crosswise into whatever width pasta you want. Unroll each cut pasta and set on a floured surface. If the pasta is too long, you can cut it into desired lengths. I once saw a video that my cousin Nancy made of her Nonna, Maria Ferranti, making

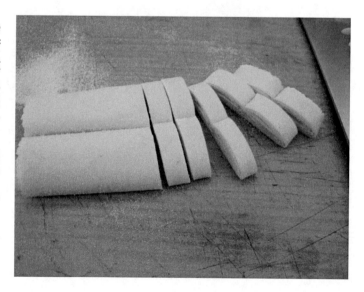

pasta. She rolled both ends of the pasta to the center and made her cuts crosswise. She then slid the knife under the pasta at the point where the two rolls met and using the backside of the knife lifted the pasta. As she lifted, the pasta very neatly unrolled. I thought this quite clever.

The pasta can be cooked and enjoyed immediately. To store fresh pasta, place it in plastic bags and refrigerate for several days or freeze for several months. If freezing pasta, do not thaw before cooking, just put the frozen pasta in boiling water. To store dried pasta, place the pasta on a table or other large surface in more-or-less a single layer until completely dry (Nonna used a bed covered with a clean sheet). Store in a box or bag.

A variation we sometimes made was spinach pasta. Here it is along with a few others. The ingredients for the pasta dough are all that differs from the basic recipe. The pasta making process is exactly the same.

Spinach Pasta

3½ c. semolina flour
1 package frozen spinach, drained, squeezed and pureed
2 large eggs
½ c. water

Tomato-Basil Pasta

3½ c. semolina flour
¼ c. tomato paste
2 Tbs. chopped fresh basil
2 large eggs
½ c. water

Lemon-Pepper Pasta

3½ c. semolina flour
1 Tbs. lemon pepper seasoning
rind of 1 lemon, grated
1 tsp. black pepper
2 Tbs. sugar
2 large eggs
½ c. fresh lemon juice

Whole-Wheat Pasta

2 c. semolina flour
1½ c. whole wheat flour
2 large eggs
¾ c. water

Zero-Cholesterol Pasta

3½ c. semolina flour
3 egg whites
2 tsp. olive oil
¾ c. water

Makes 6-8 servings

Sugo

Sugo actually means sauce and carries with it no connotation for any particular type of sauce. However, we used the word sugo to refer to my mom's red, tomato based pasta sauce. When I think back about my learning to cook, I always see a clear image of my mom and me in the kitchen making sugo. Realistically, she made the sugo while I, as her helper, cut, chopped, added and stirred. Mom never actually said, "Hey Linda, come here so I can teach you how to cook." It happened instead, by me working in the kitchen with her and having the opportunity to observe her while she cooked. I guess over time it just sort of sunk in.

There were (and still are) many afternoons that Mom had a pot of sugo simmering on the stove. The wonderful aroma filled the house tantalizing our taste buds with the pasta meal it promised later that day. Of course, it was almost impossible to walk by a pot of simmering sugo without taking a sample. So that Dad could adequately sample the sugo, he created his famed "sugo sandwich"; a slice of bread on which he spread a generous spoon of sugo. According to Dad, eating sugo on bread is probably how the Sloppy Joe got started!

3 Tbls. olive oil
1 medium onion, chopped
4 cloves garlic
1 lb. ground beef
1 lb. Italian sausage
3 28 oz. cans stewed roma style tomatoes
3 6 oz. cans Contadina tomato paste
1 lb. fresh mushrooms
⅔ c. fresh parsley leaves, chopped
3 Tbls. oregano
3 Tbls. basil
1 Tbl. thyme
1 tsp. rosemary
1 tsp. sage
3 bay leaves
1 c. dry red wine
salt and pepper to taste

Remove sausage from casing and cook in a large, heavy pot (do not use an aluminum pot, the acid in the tomatoes will react with the aluminum and the sugo will taste bad; also, you don't want to be eating aluminum!) with the ground beef until the meat is no longer pink and most of the fat has cooked out. Drain off excess fat by putting the cooked meat in a colander. Sauté the onion and garlic in the olive oil in the same pot as the meat until tender. Add the meat and continue cooking until the meat is slightly browned. Slice and add the mushrooms. Put the stewed tomatoes, one can at a time, in a blender and blend for 1-2 seconds adding each to the pot. Add the tomato paste and stir. Add the parsley, oregano, basil, thyme, rosemary, sage, bay leaves and salt and pepper. Stir well. Add the wine and stir again. Cover the sugo and simmer for about 2 hour stirring occasionally. It is important to cook the sugo at a slow simmer. Do not allow the sugo to boil at high temperatures because the tomatoes will take on a bitter, burned taste that will distort the flavor of the sugo.

Use the sugo immediately or store covered for about a week in the refrigerator. For longer storage, transfer the sugo to freezer-proof containers and freeze for up to several months.

NOTE: This recipe can be varied by one or more of the following:

- Omit the mushrooms
- Do not blender the stewed tomatoes if you want chunks of tomato in the sugo
- Use some other combination of meat(s) for example,
    - all ground beef
    - all sausage
    - sausage cut into 2" chunks
    - combination of ground beef and ground pork
    - ground turkey.
- Omit the meat for vegetarian sugo. (I served this once while my mom and dad were visiting and Dad said it was the worst sugo he had ever had!!!)

Makes about 1 gallon

Aglio Olio (Browned Butter and Garlic)

This is probably one of the most simple and delicious pasta sauces you can prepare. It can be whipped up in just a few minutes and will turn any pasta dish into a gourmet meal for family and friends. It is also great on gnocchi and ravioli. Some aglio olio recipes contain olive oil instead of butter. However this characteristically Northern Italian version features butter and cheese.

¼ lb. unsalted butter (not margarine)
3-4 cloves fresh garlic
6-8 fresh sage leaves or 1 tsp. rubbed sage
2 c. shredded Parmigiano Reggiano cheese
1 lb. spaghetti or capellini
fresh ground pepper to taste

Place pasta in plenty of boiling water and stir gently. While pasta is cooking, peel and slice the garlic lengthwise in very thin slices. Place the garlic and sage in a small skillet with the butter and melt over medium heat. Continue cooking the butter until it has a distinctively brown color, about 10-minutes, being careful not to let the butter burn. Remove from heat.

When the pasta is cooked, drain it well and put it into a pasta dish. Pour the sauce over the pasta and then put a large fork full of pasta back into the skillet and stir it around to capture all the little bits of browned butter that may still be at the bottom of the skillet. Return the 'wiping pasta' back to the pasta dish, toss and then sprinkle with 1 cup of the cheese and toss again. You can either remove the garlic and sage leaves before you pour the sauce on the pasta or leave them in with the sauce. Leaving the garlic and sage leaves is highly recommended as the garlic has a nice mellow flavor as a result of it cooking in the butter. Add another 1/2 cup of cheese and black pepper to the pasta and toss once more until the pasta is evenly coated with the sauce. Serve at once and offer the remaining 1/2 cup cheese as a garnish. This sauce's flavor is at its peak when it is fresh so enjoy immediately!!!!

Serves 6-8

Sugo Calabrase

While living in Calabria, my mom's family never added ground meat to their sugo as grinding meat was not a common practice. Instead, they made sugo by stewing chunks of meat, usually pork or chicken, in a tomato base sauce until tender. Pasta was topped with the resulting meat-flavored tomato sauce and served with one or two pieces of the stewed meat. Pecorino cheese was the usual accompaniment. After moving to the U.S. where ground meat is more available and commonly used, my Nonno Crocco continued to prefer sugo made this calabrase style and referred to pasta sauce made with ground meat as 'gravel'.

True calabrase ingredients for this sugo includes lard and water for which I have substituted olive oil and broth.

2 lb. boneless country style ribs or stewing chicken
2 Tbl. olive oil
1 medium onion
4 cloves garlic
4 c. chicken broth (or water)
2 6 oz. cans Contadina tomato paste
8 fresh basil leaves, chopped
½ c. Pecorino cheese
salt and pepper to taste

Trim any excess fat and/or skin from the meat and cut into two inch pieces if using pork, or into serving-sized pieces if using chicken. Brown the meat in 2 tablespoons of olive oil and set aside reserving 2 tablespoons of the drippings from the cooked meat. Chop the onion and garlic and sauté with the drippings in a heavy stewing pot until slightly tender. Add the meat and broth and stir. Cover the pot, bring to a simmer and cook for about 20 minutes. Add the tomato paste, basil, salt and pepper and continue simmering for 1½ hours or until the meat is tender. Remove the cover and simmer for about 30 minutes to thicken slightly. Serve over pasta accompanied by the Pecorino cheese.

Makes enough for one pound of pasta

Casonsei

Casonsei are a stuffed pasta common in Northern Italy. As a kid, we never had casonsei however, Nonna Zilioli often made them when she lived in Italy and in her earlier years in the US. During one of my mom and dad's visits to Phoenix, the conversation turned to casonsei, which for me was a big surprise because they were something I never heard of nor knew anything about. Of course, it piqued my culinary interests so that afternoon after consulting Aunt Teresa, we made a batch - it was like finding a lost treasure.

In Italy because there was little meat, Nonna's casonsei were typically made with mostly bread crumbs and cheese, occasionally also with a scant amount of sausage for flavor. Nonna's mother, Rachele, sometimes added raisins to her casonsei as a sweet treat for the children (who at the time were Uncle Jack, Aunt Teresa and my dad). My dad remembers Nonna cutting her pasta for casonsei with this one particular jelly jar that just happen to be the perfect diameter for casonsei and made from glass thin enough to easily cut through the pasta.

When ready to make casonsei, Nonna and her sisters had a little joke they would sometimes play on their kids. Pretending to forget, they would send their child to one of the aunt's house to find out what size to make the casonsei. The aunt being in on the joke would reply, "as big as your mouth".

Filling:

    1 lb. Italian sausage, casing removed
    ½ lb. ground veal or beef
    1-2 cloves garlic, pressed
    ½ c. parsley leaves, chopped
    1 tsp. rosemary
    2 eggs, beaten
    1 c. grated Parmigiano Reggiano
    2 c. bread crumbs from good quality Italian bread
    1 c. milk
    ¼ tsp. nutmeg
    salt and pepper to taste
    ½ c. raisins (optional)

Brown the meat in a heavy skillet and pour off any excess fat. Grind the meat in a food processor until finely chopped but not pureed or pasty. Transfer the meat to a large bowl. Moisten the breadcrumbs with the milk, add to the meat mixture and mix well with the remaining ingredients.

Make the pasta dough (see below) and roll it out to ⅛" thick. Cut 2½ 3" rounds with a biscuit cutter or glass. Put a spoonful of filling in the center of a pasta round, fold in half and press the edges together to seal. Lay the casonsei on the counter, seam side down, lay your index finger over the center and perpendicular to the casonsei, then press gently while lifting the ends around your finger to form a little "boat". Repeat with the remaining pasta and filling.

Cook the casonsei in salted, boiling water until the pasta is cooked through, about 10-15 minutes. Drain well, and dress with browned-butter sage sauce and cheese. Whether these casonsei are the size of your mouth or not, you will love these delicious and savory morsels.

Makes about 10 dozen

Pasta dough:
      3½ c. semolina or unbleached all-purpose flour
      2 eggs, beaten
      1 tsp. salt
      ¾ c. water

Place the flour in a large bowl. Make a well in the middle of the flour and add the eggs, salt and water. Mix well then turn onto a lightly floured work surface and knead until well mixed and smooth. Cover with a damp cloth and let the dough rest for about 30 minutes before rolling out.

Gnocchi

Gnocchi are small potato dumplings that make an elegant alternative to pasta. When made well, gnocchi are tender morsels of gastronomic delight. If made poorly, they can range from potato mush to hard, gummy dough balls. Although the point of 'made well' lays somewhere in between, finding it is nothing more than a matter of taste. The texture of the gnocchi is determined by the proportion of potato to flour so you might have to make gnocchi several times to get it just right - for you. As the ratio of potato to flour leans towards more potato, the gnocchi will become softer and not hold their shape as well. Conversely, a ratio of more flour will result in a firmer gnocchi.

When Shannon became part of my family, she was of course, introduced to gnocchi. In my family, they are served fairly regularly during family dinners and I typically make them on Christmas Eve. Being the potato fan that she is, Shannon quickly claimed gnocchi as one of her favorites and is sure to request them for any special occasion and when visiting her Nonna (my mom) in Detroit. Just weeks before her 21st birthday, Shannon decided she wanted to learn how to make gnocchi. So, on November 4, 2007 Shannon and I made gnocchi together for the first time. I can't describe the sense of wellness I felt as I watched (and participated in) my family's tradition of gnocchi making being passed on to another generation. I suppose it happened when I first learned to make gnocchi from my mother – I just didn't realize it was.

I like gnocchi to hold their shape when cooked and still have a little bite but not be doughy so, here's how Shannon and I make them.

> 4 large russet potatoes
> 1 Tbl olive oil
> 2½ - 3 c. unbleached all purpose flour plus bench flour
> 3 eggs plus 1 yolk
> 1 Tbl. salt plus extra for cooking water

Wash and scrub the potatoes, wipe dry, pierce in several places with a fork and coat with olive oil. Microwave the potatoes until just cooked, about 10-15 minutes. Remove from the microwave and cool so they can be comfortably handled. Run them though a ricer (or peel and mash with a potato masher) into a large mixing bowl. Sprinkle the potatoes with the lesser amount of flour, add 1 Tbl. salt and mix gently until the potato and flour are evenly incorporated. Whisk together the eggs and the yolk and mix into the potato-flour mixture. Fold the dough over onto itself in thirds and press in a gentle kneading-like motion, turn 90-degrees and repeat just until a cohesive dough forms.

Working on a lightly floured surface with about ¾ cup of dough at a time, roll the dough into a ½" diameter rope. Cut the rope into not quite 1" gnocchi, flouring your knife as needed to prevent sticking. Roll each gnocchi along the tines of a fork using your thumb to make a depression on one side while the tines of the fork make shallow grooves on the other. These indentations hold the sauce around the gnocchi and give them their characteristic shape. If the gnocchi seem sticky, flour lightly. Transfer them to a well floured baking sheet and continue until all of the dough has been shaped into gnocchi.

Gnocchi are best if cooked soon after they are made (within about an hour) so get a large pot of water boiling while you are shaping the gnocchi. Add salt to the boiling water and using a spatula, lift the gnocchi from the baking sheet and gently drop them into the boiling water. Cook for about 10-minutes, or until done, stirring carefully and occasionally. Some claim that the gnocchi are cooked as soon as they float to the top but I find them to still be rather raw tasting and needing further cooking. The best way to tell when they are cooked is to taste one.

When the gnocchi are cooked, lift them from the boiling water with a large slotted spoon or strainer and set them in a colander to drain thoroughly. Place the gnocchi in a large pasta serving bowl and dress with your favorite sauce. I think gnocchi are particularly good with browned-butter sage sauce and parmesan cheese however, a good tomato based spaghetti sauce is very delicious too. Enjoy.

Makes 8 servings

Lasagna

Lasagna is a popular and delicious pasta casserole consisting of wide pasta noodles layered with sauces and cheeses. There are many variations depending on the sauce, its ingredients and types of cheeses. The sauce will carry the overall taste of the lasagna so be sure and use one that is full-bodied and tasty.

I learned to make lasagna from my Nonna Zilioli. When I was in my mid-teens, my dad and I spent an afternoon at her house so that my dad could make some repairs to her furnace. She made lasagna for lunch that day and I not only had the benefit of enjoying the delicious meal she prepared, but also had an opportunity to help and observe her lasagna making techniques. She used freshly made lasagna pasta and put an interesting Northern Italian twist to the lasagna. Instead of using ricotta cheese, one of the traditional lasagna cheeses, she made a creamy, rich béchamel sauce and drizzled it among the other lasagna ingredients. It was a truly memorable lasagna.

The following recipe is a traditional, basic lasagna. For variation try adding small bite-sized meatballs, slices of cooked Italian sausage, sliced cooked eggs, cooked vegetables or like my Nonna, substitute béchamel sauce for ricotta. Regardless of the exact combination of ingredients you choose, a fresh lasagna bubbling hot from the oven is guaranteed to delight your family and guests.

> 1 lb. fresh or imported lasagna pasta
> 5-6 c. tomato based pasta sauce, with or without meat
> 1½ lb. ricotta cheese
> 1½ lb. mozzarella cheese, shredded
> ¾ c. parmesan cheese, grated

Cook the pasta until it is nearly done and drain well. Slightly warm the sauce. Cover the bottom of a 10x14" baking pan with ½ cup of the sauce. Place a single thickness of lasagna pasta over the sauce. Evenly spread about 1½ cups of the sauce on the pasta and sprinkle with ¼ cup of the parmesan cheese. Drop by evenly spaced spoonfuls, ½ pound of the ricotta cheese. Cover the layer with ½ pound of the mozzarella cheese. Place a single thickness of lasagna pasta over the first layer and repeat with sauce and cheeses, making three layers total. You should end with the mozzarella cheese. (If you have some lasagna noodles left, you can make a top layer of noodles with some sauce and parmesan cheese.)

If you are using fresh lasagna pasta, which is considerably thinner than commercial imported pasta, you will need to make more than three layers for the lasagna. Modify the above procedure so that the sauce and cheeses are proportionally divided among the layers. The additional layers of thin fresh pasta give the lasagna a wonderful, delicate texture.

In either case, tent with aluminum foil and bake at 350° for 55 minutes. Remove the aluminum foil and bake for 10-15 minutes longer to slightly brown the top. Remove from the oven and allow to cool for 10 minutes before serving.

Makes 12 servings.

NOTE: For a slightly modified version of this pasta casserole use tubular pasta like rigatoni, ziti or mostaccioli instead of the lasagna pasta. Spoon the tubular pasta more-or-less in a single thickness in place of the lasagna pasta and cover with sauce and cheeses as for lasagna.

Béchamel Sauce

2 c. milk
½ stick butter
½ c. flour
salt and pepper to taste

Melt the butter in a medium saucepan and add the flour. Mix together to form a roux and stir over medium heat for a couple minutes. Add the milk to the roux while stirring constantly to form a smooth sauce. Add the salt and pepper, bring the béchamel to a slow boil and cook for 10-15 minutes stirring periodically.

The béchamel should be just thick enough to coat the backside of a spoon. If too thick, add a little more milk. If too thin, whisk some flour and water together, adding the water a little at a time until a smooth, pourable paste forms. While briskly stirring the hot béchamel with the whisk, slowing add some of the flour and water mixture, a little at a time, until the béchamel is the desired consistency.

Ravioli

These small, stuffed envelopes of pasta are one of my very favorite pasta dishes. In fact, they are probably one of my all-time favorite Italian dishes. Although meat and cheese ravioli have rather different tastes, both are equally delicious and always make a special meal.

> 1 recipe homemade pasta
> 1 recipe either meat or ricotta filling
> 5 c. spaghetti sauce
> ½ c. grated Parmesan cheese
> 3 Tbl. salt

Roll (or use a pasta machine) about ¼ of the pasta into a round 1/16" thick. Beginning 2" from the edge of the round that is closest to you, place rounded teaspoons of the filling, in a line, ¾-1" apart. Each spoonful will become one ravioli. Fold the 2" edge of pasta over the filling so there is a ½" overlap on the side opposite the fold. Seal this long edge by pressing slightly with your fingers. To seal the sides, start in the middle of the row, and lay your index finger between the ravioli pressing slightly. Be sure the ravioli are well sealed on all the unfolded sides. Work your way to the ends of the row, pushing any excess air out from between the pasta and filling as you go. (If you start at the ends and work towards the center, air will get trapped in your ravioli. The air

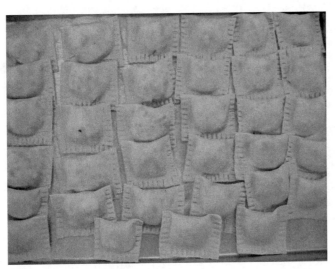

will expand as the ravioli cook, which can cause the pasta to burst). Using a ravioli or pastry cutter, make a cut lengthwise along the overlapping edge and then cut each ravioli away from one another. Seal the edges again with the tines of a fork. (Some ravioli cutters do this as they cut the ravioli. If you have such a cutter you may not need to seal with the fork). Lift each ravioli from your work surface and set them on a floured, cookie sheet. Place another line of filling about 2" from the edge of the remaining pasta round and repeat until the round is used. Roll each remaining portion of pasta and repeat the process.

To cook the ravioli, bring two gallons of water to a boil in a large pot. Add the salt and carefully drop the ravioli, a few at a time, into the water. Gently stir the ravioli periodically and continue boiling until the pasta is cooked, about 10-12 minutes. Lift the ravioli from the pot with a large slotted scooping utensil and place the ravioli in a colander to drain. Do not dump the ravioli directly from the pot of boiling water into the colander since they may break. Layer the ravioli and warmed spaghetti sauce in a shallow baking dish, and mix slightly. Cover the dish with aluminum foil and bake in a preheated 375° oven for 20 minutes. Remove the aluminum foil and garnish with Parmesan cheese. Serve.

For a delicious variation, try ravioli with browned butter sauce instead of spaghetti sauce.

NOTE: To store the ravioli, place cookie sheets of uncooked ravioli in the freezer. When frozen (20-30 minutes), remove the ravioli from the cookie sheets and place in freezer bags. The bags of ravioli can be kept frozen for several months. Do not thaw the ravioli before cooking, just drop them into the boiling water frozen. Your cooking time may be a little longer.

Makes about 6 dozen

Stuffed Pasta

Manicotti and stuffed shells are two common stuffed pastas that except for the shape of the pasta, are virtually the same dish. Ravioli is another delicious stuffed pasta whose preparation method is sufficiently different from manicotti and stuffed shells that it is covered in a separate recipe.

Manicotti and stuffing shell pasta can be purchased at most grocery stores. However, manicotti can easily be made from homemade pasta by cutting the pasta into a 4-inch square into which the filling is rolled.

> 18 manicotti pasta or 24 large stuffing shell pasta
> 3-4 c. tomato based pasta sauce
> 1 recipe ricotta cheese filling
> ½ c. Parmesan cheese, grated

Cook the pasta until nearly done and drain well (if using fresh pasta it does not need to be cooked). While the pasta is cooling, evenly spread almost half of the pasta sauce in a baking dish large enough to hold the manicotti or shells. When the pasta is cool enough to handle, stuff each manicotti or shell with the ricotta filling and place in the baking dish. The manicotti are a little more difficult to stuff and you may need to use a butter knife or similarly shaped utensil to push the filling to the middle of the manicotti. Or, use a pastry bag or ziplock bag with the tip cut out. Do not over-fill the pasta since the filling expands somewhat while cooking. Continue until all the pasta are filled. Spoon the remaining sauce over the top of the manicotti or shells. Cover the baking dish with aluminum foil and bake at 350° for 45-minutes. Serve garnished with the Parmesan cheese.

Makes 6-8 servings.

Ricotta Cheese Filling

Ricotta cheese filling is a light yet flavorful cheese filling that is used for stuffed pasta dishes like ravioli, manicotti and stuffed shells.

> 1 lb. ricotta cheese
> 3 large eggs
> 3 cloves fresh garlic, pressed
> ¾ c. fresh parsley leaves, chopped
> ½ c. parmesan cheese, grated
> ¼ c. bread crumbs
> 1 Tbl. oregano
> salt and pepper to taste
> 1 package frozen spinach, drained and chopped (optional)

Thoroughly mix all ingredients and use immediately or refrigerate, covered for up to two days.

Meat Filling for Ravioli

Making meat filling for ravioli is somewhat time consuming however, the filling can be made ahead and stored for several days in the refrigerator. I am sure that once you taste the scrumptious ravioli made from this filling you will undoubtedly think the time well worth the effort.

4 large pork chops
¾ lb. veal or dark turkey
6 cloves pressed, fresh garlic
2 tsp. rosemary
1 Tbl. thyme
½ tsp. ground sage
1 Tbl. oregano
½ c. dry white wine
3 Tbl. olive oil
1 c. parmesan cheese
¾ c. bread crumbs
1 package frozen spinach, thawed
¾ c. fresh parsley, chopped
3 eggs
salt and pepper

Mix together three cloves of garlic, rosemary, sage, thyme and black pepper. Rub onto the pork chops and veal/turkey. Heat the olive oil in a large, heavy skillet and slightly brown the meat on all sides. Add the white wine, cover and simmer for about 15 minutes. Remove the lid and cook off any remaining liquid.

When the meat is cool enough to handle, remove from bones and discard any fat and skin. Chop the meat in a food processor until it is similar in texture to ground beef. Place the chopped meat in a large mixing bowl with the eggs, bread crumbs, parmesan cheese, oregano, remaining garlic and parsley. Squeeze the excess water from the spinach and chop finely in the food processor. Add to the meat mixture. Salt and pepper to taste. Using your hand, thoroughly mix the meat mixture.

Polenta

All About Polenta

Although polenta is cornmeal cooked in salted water, it should never be considered mere cornmeal mush. Polenta is the staple of the Bergamas' diet, and to them, is life itself. Because it serves so beautifully as a vehicle for many different toppings and sauces, it is an interesting and versatile food.

Polenta ranges from a breakfast food of hot cereal when topped with milk and sugar to an elegant main course when served with mui, a rich, meaty cream sauce.

In Bergamo each household had a polenta pot in which to cook the day's polente (yes, there were often more than one). The polenta pot is a large cast iron pot with a rounded bottom and a handle to hang the pot over the fireplace. A long, sturdy stick somewhat oval in cross section, called a tarrel, is used to stir the polenta as it cooks. When prepared on an open fire, a well-cooked polenta must be stirred nearly constantly to prevent scorching or burning which will most assuredly ruin an otherwise good polenta. With modern gas and electric stoves the need for constant stirring is not as critical however, during her entire life of polenta making, my Nonna Margherita never abandoned the constant stirring aspect of polenta cooking.

Basic Polenta

Polenta served with mui seems to be everyone's overwhelming favorite. The cornmeal milling will affect the texture of your polenta so try some different ones for a pleasant variation.

2 quarts water
3 cups cornmeal
1 Tbl salt

Bring the water to a rolling boil in a heavy, metal pot with enough room to comfortably stir the polenta. Add the salt. While stirring vigorously, slowly mix or whisk the cornmeal into the boiling water. Cook on medium-low heat for about 40 minutes stirring frequently with a tarrel or sturdy wooden spoon. The polenta stirring motion should be more similar to folding than to true stirring.

When done, the polenta will pull away from the sides of the pot and should be somewhat soft but able to hold its shape. Turn the polenta out onto a large platter and serve immediately with your favorite sauce.

For an alternate cooking method to avoid lumping, add the cornmeal to cold, salted water and bring to a boil while stirring constantly. Or, mix the cornmeal with some of the water and mix the cornmeal-water mixture into the remaining boiling, salted water. Polenta ingredients can also be placed in a casserole and baked covered for 1 hour at 350°. Varieties of instant polenta meals have recently come to market and although they are not quite as flavorful and robust as a cooked polenta, they are a good alternative when one needs a polenta in a hurry.

Dessert Polenta

If one could possibly have room for dessert after a delicious meal of polenta and mui, this is a not-too-sweet, simple and tasty treat. It takes advantage of the dinner elements probably still on the table and illustrates the versatility of this fundamental food.

> 1 serving polenta
> 2-3 tsp. sugar
> ¼ c. red wine

Place the polenta on a plate and flatten slightly with the back of a fork. Sprinkle with sugar and then top with the red wine.

Fried Polenta

Fried polenta is an excellent way to serve leftover polenta. The thin crispy 'crust' is a nice touch and in fact, is Uncle Al's favorite way to have polenta. Although leftover mui is a good accompaniment for fried polenta it is commonly served with melted cheese.

> 8 slices leftover polenta ½" thick
> 3 Tbls. vegetable oil
> 2 Tbls. butter
> 1½ c. shredded Munster or Fontina cheese

Heat a large, non-stick skillet to medium-high. Add the vegetable oil and evenly arrange the polenta slices in the hot oil. Cook until browned, about 7-minutes, then flip the slices and brown the other side.

While the polenta slices are browning, melt the butter in a second, smaller skillet. Add the shredded cheese in 2-3 portions stirring in between additions. Continue stirring on low heat until cheese is melted.

Place the browned polenta slices on a platter (or four separate plates), salt and pepper to taste and top with the melted cheese.

Serves 4

NOTE: The cuisine of rural Southern US has a dish almost identical to fried polenta that is served for breakfast with butter and syrup. Give it a try.

Morning Breakfast Polenta

Because polenta is a staple food, it was typically cooked and eaten multiple times a day. A morning breakfast polenta was eaten in very much the same way we might have oatmeal or other hot cooked cereal.

> 1 c. water
> ½ tsp. salt
> ⅓ c. cornmeal
> 1 tsp. butter
> 2 tsp. sugar
> ⅓ c. warm milk

Bring the water to a boil, add the salt and whisk in the cornmeal. Cook the polenta for about 30 minutes or until done, stirring occasionally. Transfer the polenta to a bowl and top with the butter, sugar and warm milk. Then, go have yourself a great day!!!!

NOTE: Depending on how thick or loose you like your polenta, you can add or omit some of the cornmeal.

Polenta Calabrase

Unlike northern Italy, polenta is not a staple food of southern Italy. Nonetheless, it was occasionally eaten by my mother's family in Calabria. This version (compared to polenta and mui) is an excellent illustration of the diversity in southern and northern Italian cuisine.

4 c. tomato based spaghetti sauce (sugo)
3 c. water
1 c. corn meal
⅓ c. grated Pecorino cheese
1 tsp. salt

Place the water, 2 cups of sugo, the corn meal and salt in a large heavy pot, mix well and bring to a simmer while stirring. Cover and cook for about 25 minutes on medium-low, stirring occasionally. While the polenta is cooking, heat the remaining sugo to a simmer.

When the polenta is cooked, turn it onto a, shallow serving dish and make a well in the center. Top with the sugo and garnish with Pecorino cheese.

Makes 4-6 servings

The Making of a Polenta Dinner

Aunt Teresa's polenta dinners were one of our family favorites – they are truly classic. After arriving to her house and engaging is some conversation and helping with the last minute details, we all made our way down to the basement where a beautiful and inviting dinner table awaits. It usually went something like this:

The table is set and ready to accept the anticipating diners. Each setting is ready with a generous serving of polenta. Uncle Al is making sure that all is in order.

The guests select their seats and start the meal. The little boy in the high-chair at the end of the table is my nephew, Luke. My Mom is getting him situated. Larry and my Dad are at the left of the table. On the right hand side of the table starting from the back of the room is Aunt Pauline, Danny, Dave, Sara and Uncle Al.

Guests enjoy their meal in an atmosphere of conversation, debate and laughter. Aunt Teresa (front left) and Joan converse while Bill (standing left) is thinking about having seconds. Notice my Mom trying to get Luke to eat more!!!!

This particular meal was especially significant because it is where Luke eats his very first polenta – he truly becomes a Zilioli.

and so on and on…

Risotto

Family Classic Risotto

Risotto – derived from the word "riso" which means, "rice" in Italian – is a tasty and satisfying dinner entrée that my mom often served. Although every cuisine of the world has its own rice dishes, Italian risotto is characterized by a creamy, soft texture that develops as starch is released from the rice kernel during the traditional risotto cooking process. For good results, hot liquid should be added to the risotto in small batches giving the rice kernels time to absorb the liquid between each addition. Nearly continuous stirring is also important to coax the starch out of the rice kernels and into the risotto. It would be accurate to say, risotto is more of a cooking method rather than a specific set of ingredients so there are literally hundreds of different types of risottos.

My mom usually made a lightly tomato flavored risotto seasoned with chicken broth, aromatics, and finely chopped and browned chicken gizzards. After she cooked together all that goodness, mom stirred in a generous sprinkling of grated Parmesan cheese, butter and parsley then, to our delight, delivered the lusciously creamy risotto to the table.

My dad really likes rice, so risotto is one of his favorite meals and during one of those meals when I was still just a young girl, he taught me the optimal method for eating risotto. Here is a recap of his instructions:

Place several spoonfuls of risotto on the middle of a dinner plate.

1. Using the backside of your fork, push the risotto into a flat, even round not quiet ½ inch thick. This increases the surface area so the risotto can cool to a comfortable eating temperature more quickly.

2. Eat a swath, exactly the width of your fork through the middle of the round so that the round of risotto is left in two semi-circles. This allows further cooling while still allowing enjoyment of the risotto.

3. Eat a second swath through the middle of the round, perpendicular to the first swath, so that the round of risotto is left in 4 quarter-circles. The risotto should now be at the perfect temperature.

4. Eat each quarter, one at a time. Perfection.

Arborio rice is most popular for risotto but any short grain variety can be used instead. Short grain brown rice adds a little more chew and nutty flavor but will not develop the same degree of creaminess and takes about three times as long to cook.

2 c. Arborio or other variety of short-grain rice
4 Tbl. olive oil
1 c. dry white wine
5-6 c. chicken broth, steaming hot
1 medium onion, chopped
2 gloves garlic, peeled and chopped
½ lb. finely chopped chicken gizzards
OR   ½ lb. Italian sausage, casing removed
3 oz. tomato paste
3 Tbl. butter
⅓ c. chopped fresh parsley
1 c. grated Parmesan cheese
salt and pepper to taste

Put the chicken broth in a pot on the stove and keep it hot during the entire cooking process. Once you start adding liquid to the rice, be sure to keep stirring.

Heat the olive oil in a Dutch oven (or similar cooking vessel) and add the onions and garlic. Sauté until just starting to soften then add the chopped gizzards (or sausage) and stir occasionally until browned. Add the rice and let it cook in the hot oil for about 2-3-minutes stirring often - you will see a slight translucent "shine" form on the rice kernels. Season with salt and pepper.

Add the white wine and stir the risotto until nearly all the wine is absorbed. Stir in the tomato paste and about 1cup hot chicken broth – stir the risotto until the broth is absorbed. Keep adding about 1 cup of hot chicken broth at a time letting the rice absorb the broth between additions. Continue until the rice is cooked, about 20 minutes. Remember to stir the risotto often – you should see a creamy texture develop as the rice kernels expand and release their starches. The risotto should be soft and moist, so use your judgment as to whether the full 6 cups of broth is needed or if you need to add a little more broth or water. Gently mix in the butter, chopped parsley, and ½ cup of the Parmesan cheese. Serve immediately with the remaining ½ cup cheese on the side and be sure to eat the risotto the optimal method described above!

4-6 servings

Milanese Risotto

Milanese Risotto is a meaty risotto flavored with aromatics typical of northern Italian cuisine. This recipe calls for Italian sausage but any ground meat (or combination) can be substituted. Like all risottos, the traditional cooking method of stirring small amounts of hot liquid into the cooking rice is important for developing the risotto's creaming texture (see Classic Family Risotto for cooking method detail).

1 lb. Italian sausage, casing removed
2 c. Arborio or other variety of short-grain rice
1 c. dry white wine
5-6 c. chicken broth, steaming hot
1 glove garlic, peeled and chopped
1 tsp. dried thyme
½ tsp. dried sage
½ tsp. dried rosemary
5 Tbl. butter
1 c. grated Parmesan cheese
dusting of grated nutmeg
pinch of saffron, soaked in 2 Tbls water (optional)
salt and pepper to taste

Put the chicken broth in a pot on the stove and keep it hot during the entire cooking process. Once you start adding liquid to the rice, be sure to keep stirring.

Lightly brown the Italian sausage in a Dutch oven (or similar cooking vessel) while breaking up the sausage into bite-sized chunks. Drain off any excess fat then add 2 tablespoons of the butter, the rice, garlic, thyme, sage and rosemary. Stir together and cook for about 2-3-minutes stirring often - you will see a slight translucent "shine" form on the rice kernels. Season with salt and pepper.

Add the white wine and stir the risotto until nearly all the wine is absorbed. Next, add about 1cup hot chicken broth and the saffron, if using; stir the risotto until the broth is absorbed. Keep adding about 1 cup of hot chicken broth at a time letting the rice absorb the broth between additions. Continue until the rice is cooked - about 20 minutes. Remember to stir the risotto often – you should see a creamy texture develop as the rice kernels expand and release their starches. The risotto should be soft and moist, so use your judgment as to whether the full 6 cups of broth is needed or if you need to add a little more broth or water. Gently mix in the remaining 3 tablespoons of butter, ½ cup of the Parmesan cheese, and dusting of nutmeg. Serve immediately with the remaining ½ cup cheese on the side.

4-6 servings

Eggs

Frittata

Frittata refers to a style of cooking eggs the beauty of which, is that once you master this easy cooking method, the varieties are endless, and limited only by your imagination. Unlike an omelet where the fillings are folded inside a sheet of cooked eggs, frittata's fillings are mixed and cooked together with the eggs. Frittatas are delicious, quick and nutritious and can be tailored to any meal or occasion by varying the filling with different combinations of vegetables, cheeses and/or meats. Here is a classic:

> 10 eggs
> 2 c. cooked spinach or other greens drained and chopped
> ½ c. grated parmesan cheese
> 3 Tbl. butter or olive oil or combination
> salt and pepper to taste

Break the eggs into a large bowl, add salt and pepper to taste, and mix well. Heat the butter or olive oil on medium heat in a 12", non-stick frying pan, add the spinach, salt and pepper, and stir. Heat until the spinach is heated through.

Pour the egg mixture over the spinach and sprinkle with the cheese. Using a heat resistant rubber spatula, carefully pull the eggs from the sides of the pan and mix gently in the center. Continue working the eggs from the edges and lifting slightly from the pan so some of the uncooked eggs can run underneath. The frittata should be a single "cake" of cooked egg

and spinach, but not over cooked on the bottom to where the eggs are dark browned and rubbery.

When the frittata starts to take form, flip it over by placing a dinner plate upside-down over the frittata. Assuming you're right handed - hold the plate firmly in place with your right hand and lift the pan with your left then flip the pan and plate simultaneously so the frittata is turned out onto the plate. Place the pan back on the stove and slide the frittata back into the pan so its un-cooked side is now in the bottom of the pan. Cook for about a minute longer, shaking the pan several times so the frittata doesn't stick to the pan. Slide the frittata onto a large plate or serving dish. Cut into wedges and serve. My dad likes a little red wine vinegar sprinkled on his frittatas - go ahead and give it a try.

Serves 4

VARIATIONS:
- sautéed bell pepper, onions and cooked Italian sausage with mozzarella cheese
- cooked zucchini with oregano
- cooked asparagus with garlic and fresh sage
- cooked broccoli with cheddar cheese
- sautéed mushrooms with thyme
- substitute Egg Beaters or egg whites for the whole eggs

Zabaglione

Zabaglione is a well know Italian pudding-like dessert that is sometimes flavored with liquors or citrus zests. When my Dad was going to trade school, Nonna Zilioli sometimes made him zabaglione when he came home for lunch which he ate by dipping pieces of bread into its warm goodness.

> 4 egg yolks
> 4 tsp. sugar
> 4 Tbl. marsala, white wine or other sweet liquor

Place the egg yolks and sugar in the top of a small double boiler and whisk vigorously (or use an electric hand mixer) until the eggs start to turn pale yellow and frothy. Place the pot over, but not in, slightly boiling water. Continue whisking until the zabaglione has thickened and is light and fluffy, about 3-minutes. Stir in the marsala (or other flavoring) and cook for about 2 minutes more. You may have to lift the top of the double boiler off and back over the boiling water to prevent the eggs from curdling. When done, zabaglione should be the consistency of a soft mousse.

Spoon into small, stemmed glasses and serve warm or chilled. Just before serving, you can lace with a small amount of liquor or top with a small dollop of whipped cream. Zabaglione can also be served as a topping for fresh fruit or berries.

Serves 2

Eggs with Sage and Butter

This is how my Nonna Zilioli cooked eggs - the flavors are classic Northern Italian.

>2 Tbl. butter
>3-4 fresh sage leaves
>2 large eggs
>salt and pepper

Place the butter and sage leaves in a small skillet and heat on medium. Cook until the butter is slightly browned and the sage leaves are wilted and fragrant. Crack the eggs into the hot butter, salt and pepper to taste, and cook to your personal preference.

Place the eggs on a plate (the sage leaves will probably be cooked into the bottom of the eggs) and pour the butter over the top. These are delicious with toasted slices of Italian bread.

NOTE: The sage leaves can be cut or torn into pieces if desired. If fresh sage is not available, dried sage can be used instead.

Egg Sbattuto

Egg sbattuto was one of my most favorite breakfasts. My mom didn't make it very often but when she did, it delighted me to be having this wonderful treat. I remember eating it slowly, savoring every bite, so I could make it last as long as possible.

My Nonna Zilioli sometimes made an 8-10 egg sbattuto (she used whole eggs) with milk for the family dinner serving it in bowls spooned over a plain, baking soda bread/cake she sometimes made.

Egg sbattuto is simply egg yolks mixed with sugar until light and creamy - essentially the begins of egg nog (which by the way, is also something I love). Because eggs were not abundant in Italy, their nutrient richness was reserved primarily for children or the infirm and fed to them by mixing egg sbattuto with milk. On occasion, my mom and her sister enjoyed egg sbattuto mixed with an espresso or caffe latte.

> 1 egg yolk
> 1 tsp. sugar

Place the egg yolk and sugar in a small, rounded bottom cup. Mix vigorously with a teaspoon until light yellow in color and falling in ribbons from the spoon. This is delicious eaten as is or mixed with a cup of milk or caffe latte.

Main Dishes

Baccala

In Italy, a region heavily influenced by Catholicism, meals associated with religious holidays traditionally followed the Friday-fasting practice of not eating meat. Consequently, like many Italian families whose Christmas Eve meal centered around seafood, my Mom's family celebrated Christmas Eve with a meal of fried baccala (dried cod).

Drying the cod, a method of preservation, imparts a unique flavor and firm texture to the fish. The Italian markets we frequented in Detroit always displayed piles of baccala - large whole fish, flattened and dried - in large baskets. As a child I thought they were so curious and didn't understand how these seemingly dry, stiff what-ever-they-were could possibly be eaten.

What I didn't realize is baccala must be soaked in water for several days before cooking where it transforms into its characteristic firm, meaty fillets. Evidently some of the merchants in Falerna - my Mom's native town - sold baccala pre-soaked so they could be cooked and eaten that same day. I leaned this small fact about life in Falerna when my Nonna and Nonno Crocco once got into a huge argument as to whether one of their favorite street vendors sold his baccala dried or already soaked. I guess we learn from our families in many different ways.

In Calabria, baccala was fried in olive oil but because olive oil smokes at low temperatures, mixing it with vegetable oil will prevent smoking while retaining classic olive oil flavor. There is no need to salt the fillets since they will already be mildly salty.

> 1½ lbs. dried baccala
> ½ c. all purpose flour
> 3 large eggs
> 3½ c. seasoned dry bread crumbs
> 1½ c. oil for frying - 1 c. vegetable oil and ½ c. olive oil
> 1 lemon cut into wedges (optional)

Place the baccala into a large bowl or dish with enough cold water to cover the baccala by about an inch. Cover and store in the refrigerator for several days changing the water 2-3 times daily until the fillets are reconstituted. Drain off the water and lay the fillets on several layers of paper towels to drain completely. Pat any remaining water from the baccala and cut the fillets into serving sizes about 3-4" square.

Put the flour and bread crumbs on separate plates or in shallow bowls (pie plates works perfectly). Thoroughly beat the three eggs in a bowl large enough to fit a fillet. Working with one fillet at a time, coat the fillet with flour and shake off the excess. Dip into the egg mixture then place on the plate with the bread crumbs. Coat the fillet with bread crumbs, pressing them slightly onto the fillet then gently shake off excess. Place on a wire rack in a single layer.

Heat the oil in a frying pan or sauté pan to 325°-350°. Place several fillets in the pan so they are not crowded and cook until nicely browned on the bottom. Carefully flip them over, and brown the other side. Remove from the oil and keep the fillets warm while draining on paper towels. Continue cooking until all the baccala is cooked. Arrange on a serving platter with lemon wedges, if using. For a traditional Christmas Eve meal, serve with linguine aglio olio.

Serves 4-6

Chicken Cutlets

Chicken Cutlets are so universally loved, that I can say with certainty, that they are loved by literally everyone. Whether at family gatherings, dinners at home, or picnics at the beach, a big plate of chicken cutlets were popular fare with our family. Their versatility makes them perfect for an elegant meal, a practical family week-day dinner, or a casual lunch of sandwiches (a great way to use leftovers). Chicken Cutlets are my daughter's favorite meal - especially when served with gnocchi aglio olio - and something I make nearly every year for her birthday. When I married Ray, I even went as far as to alter my family's traditional Christmas Eve meal of fried baccala and replace it with Chicken Cutlets as I was certain that his young daughters would turn their noses to fish, but would love the chicken cutlets - I was right.

Typically - and my family being no exception - chicken cutlets are dredged in seasoned, dried bread crumbs which I admit, results in perfectly respectable and delicious chicken cutlets. My version of seasoning the cutlets and using fresh bread crumbs instead, I believe elevates this already scrumptious chicken dish to culinary nirvana.

> 4 skinless, boneless chicken breasts
> 2-3 cloves fresh garlic
> 2 Tbl. fresh rosemary
> 1 Tbl. fresh thyme
> 4-5 leaves fresh sage
> ½ c. all purpose flour
> 2 large eggs
> 3 c. fresh bread crumbs (recipe below)
> 1 c. oil for frying - ¾ c. vegetable oil and ¼ c. olive oil
> 1 lemon cut in wedges (optional)
> salt and pepper

Cut each chicken breasts crosswise into three pieces and pound each piece into a cutlet between ½" and ¼" thick. Finely chop together the garlic, rosemary, thyme and sage. Rub a pinch (about ⅛ teaspoon) of the herb mixture, and salt and pepper on each side of the cutlets and set aside.

Put the flour and bread crumbs on separate plates or in shallow bowls (pie plates works perfectly). Thoroughly beat the two eggs in a bowl large enough to fit a cutlet. Working with one cutlet at a time, coat the cutlet with flour and shake off the excess. Dip into the egg mixture then place on the plate with the bread crumbs. Coat the cutlet with bread crumbs, gently shake off excess then place the cutlet between the palms of your hands and gently press the crumbs onto the cutlet. Don't press so hard that you smash the bread crumbs but hard enough that they form to the cutlet. Place on a wire rack in a single layer.

Heat the oil in a frying pan or sauté pan to 325°-350°. Place several cutlets in the pan so they are not crowded and cook until nicely browned on the bottom. Carefully flip them over, and brown the other side. Remove from the oil and keep the cutlets warm while draining on paper towels. Continue cooking until all the cutlets are cooked. Arrange on a serving platter with lemon wedges, if using. If you're lucky enough to have leftovers, chicken cutlets make excellent sandwiches.

Makes 6-8 servings

Fresh Bread Crumbs:
For each cup of bread crumbs, whirl 4 slices of good quality white bread in a food processor.

Chicken Parmesan:
Follow the recipe for chicken cutlets. Dip each cooked cutlet into your favorite tomato sauce and place in a baking dish slightly overlapping like shingles on a roof. Ladle more sauce over the cutlets and top with parmesan or romano, and mozzarella cheese. Cover with aluminum foil and bake at 350° for about 25 minutes. Remove the foil and bake 5-10 minutes longer until the cheese is slightly browned and bubbly.

Chicken Ciaccatore

Chicken stewed in a rich, tomato sauce is one of many ways to prepare chicken. We sometimes made our sugo (spaghetti sauce) with chicken and served the tender chicken pieces atop spaghetti tossed with the tomato sauce. Chicken Ciaccatore (ciaccatore being the "hunter") builds on this concept with the addition of herbs, vegetables and wine. There is really no single or "right" way to make Chicken Ciaccatore - this particular recipe has a light tomato sauce with lots of vegetables but by all means, adjust it to suit your palate.

1 large chicken, cleaned and cut-up
1 lb. fresh italian sausage cut into 2" pieces
2 cloves fresh garlic, chopped
1 medium onion, chopped into ½" pieces
1 bell pepper cut into 1" square pieces
¾ lb. whole fresh mushrooms cleaned and stems trimmed
1 28 oz. can whole tomatoes
1 c. dry white wine
½ tsp. rosemary
1 tsp. thyme
1 Tbl. oregano or basil or combination
2 bay leaves
¼ c. coarsely chopped fresh parsley
3 Tbl. olive oil
salt and pepper

In a heavy dutch oven, lightly brown the sausage then the chicken in batches. Discard any excess drippings from the sausage. Add the olive oil, garlic, onion and bell pepper - salt and pepper then cook, stirring occasionally, until the vegetables are just beginning to soften - about 5 minutes. Return the chicken and sausage to the pot and add the white wine. Cut the tomatoes into pieces and add along with the canning juices. Season with the rosemary, thyme, oregano/basil, bay leaves, and salt and pepper to taste. Cover, and simmer on low heat for 35 minutes stirring several times. Add the mushrooms, and continue cooking uncovered for about 15 more minutes. Stir in the fresh parsley and remove from heat. Chicken Ciaccatore is delicious served with cooked tube shaped pasta like mostaccioli or rigatoni, or with polenta.

Makes 4-6 servings

VARIATIONS:
- For a thicker tomato sauce, add a can of tomato paste with the canned tomatoes
- If you want a smooth tomato sauce, run the canned tomatoes through a blender for a few seconds before adding to the pot. Or, use all canned tomato sauce.
- For some zip, add crushed red pepper with the garlic, onion and bell pepper.
- Add more or fewer vegetables as desired. Fresh fennel is a nice addition.
- I've seen Chicken Ciaccatore served over rice, but this doesn't seem Italian to me.

Meatballs

No one would argue the meatball's place as an icon of Italian-American cuisine.   Ironically, in Italy, large amounts of meat and especially ground meat, were not used in cooking.   Meat was used sparingly - more as flavoring than the main event.   However, when my family came to the US where they found new or an abundance of what in Italy were scarce ingredients, my Nonna Crocco adapted her cooking style to take advantage of these offerings and in doing so, fully embraced the meatball as an Americanized style of her Italian cooking.

Nonna always cooked on a grand scale preparing not just copious amounts for our family meals but enough to also send a grocery bag of leftovers home with everyone. She counted everything she made so would know that she had fashioned 123 ravioli or baked 234 pizzelle. So, it's no surprise that her meatballs followed these same culinary principles and were monster, tennis ball sized. It would be an understatement to say they were big, but even more impressive was the delight of biting into their moist and tender deliciousness from atop a plate of pasta adorned with grated cheese.

Many meatball recipes including Nonna's, call for equal parts ground beef, pork and veal however, meatballs can be made from any type of ground meat or combination there of.

> 1 lb. each ground beef, pork and veal
> 3½ c. Italian bread cut in ½" cubes
> 1 c. grated parmesan cheese
> 4 eggs
> 2 Tbl. fresh garlic, finely chopped (about 4 cloves)
> ½ c. fresh parsley leaves, chopped
> 2 Tbl. dried oregano
> 1 tsp. each thyme and rosemary, fresh chopped or dried
> 1 Tbl. salt and 1 tsp. pepper or to taste
> ½ c. olive oil

Moisten the bread cubes with about ½ cup warm water and break them up between your fingers. Place the moistened bread and all the other ingredients, except the olive oil, into a large bowl and mix well (its totally fine to use your hands as they are the best meatball mixing utensil out there). Using about ⅓ cup of the mixture at a time, shape into balls (if you're like my Nonna who prefers giant meatballs, use more).

Heat the olive oil in a large pan and cook the meatballs in batches, turning several times so they are browned on all sides. They may not be cooked all the way through, but that's okay. Remove from the pan and carefully drop into a pot of simmering sugo (tomato sauce for pasta). Simmer for about 1-hour stirring very gingerly several times. Dish the meatballs on top of a large serving platter of cooked pasta that has been tossed in the sugo and topped with fresh, grated cheese.

Makes about 2 dozen

NOTE: Instead of frying the meatballs, place them in a shallow baking pan in a single layer and bake at 425° for about 25-30 minutes or until browned.

Mui

Mui is a deliciously rich sauce that is a classic accompaniment to polenta. My Aunt Teresa served polenta with mui during the many family dinners she hosted and I do not know of anyone who has eaten it that does not love this lusty dish.

My dad warns that when eating polenta with mui you must be sure to guard yourself against falling victim to the dreaded polenta-mui cycle. That is where you need a bit more mui to finish your polenta but you take a bit too much; so you need a bit more polenta to finish your mui but you take a bit too much; so you need a bit more mui and so on. I have often wondered if Dad's falling into the cycle is really accidental.

> 3 lbs. pork roast cut into 1½" cubes
> 1 lb. veal roast or Italian sausage cut into 1½" cubes
> ¼ lb. unsalted butter
> ¼ c. sprigs of fresh rosemary or 3 Tbsp. dried
> 10-12 fresh, whole sage leaves or 1 Tb. dried
> 1½ c. dry white wine
> ¾ c. chicken broth
> 2 c. heavy or whipping cream
> 2 Tbsp. flour
> salt and pepper

Melt the butter in a heavy skillet large enough to not crowd the meat. If your skillet is not large enough, cook the meat in several batches. Add the meat, rosemary and sage and brown thoroughly on medium-high heat turning the meat several times. Salt and pepper to taste. The meat and drippings should be a rich, dark brown but not burnt. Be sure to allow sufficient browning since the dark browning of the meat and butter is key to the wonderful flavor of this sauce.

Once the meat is browned, add the wine and deglaze the pan. Lift the meat from the pan, one piece at a time, being careful that the rosemary and sage does not adhere to the meat, and place into a dutch oven or heavy pot.

Strain the deglazed mixture into the pot with the meat.

Return the herbs in the strainer to the original skillet, add the chicken broth and allow to simmer about 2-minutes. Strain the broth into the pot with the meat. Put the herbs into a tea ball or tie in cheese cloth and add to the pot with the meat. The straining process will result in a smooth sauce which is nicely flavored with the herbs. Cover the pot and simmer for about 2½ hours or until the meat is tender. (The mui can be made ahead to this point then warmed and completed just prior to serving.)

When the meat is cooked, add the cream and bring to a low simmer. Do not over boil the cream since it will separate under high heat. Mix the flour with some hot water to form a smooth paste that will pour easily. While stirring, add the flour mixture to the mui and simmer about 10 more minutes. Serve with polenta so you can sop up every single drop.

NOTE: For brown mui, follow the steps above but do not finish with the cream. Add the flour mixture to thicken the mui slightly and serve with polenta.

Serves 10-12

Roast Pork

Pork was commonly used by my family for the rich flavor that it imparts to foods, and is found braised or stewed in many of our traditional recipes. Undoubtedly, this reflects our family's heritage as farmers and their reliance on "the hog" as an important food product. It was customary for my mom's family in Calabria, to butcher two hogs each winter providing them with a source of meat, sausage, salami and lard throughout the year.

Roast pork is not only tasty and elegant, but is easy to prepare. Older recipes call for cooking pork until well done which in my opinion renders the meat dry, tough and bland. With modern farming and processing methods, the fear of trichinosis is no longer a concern and we are free to enjoy pork roasted to juicy perfection. Left-overs make great sandwiches or a hearty addition to a crisp, green salad.

3 lbs. pork loin roast or pork tenderloin(s)
4-5 cloves garlic
1 Tbl. each fresh rosemary and thyme
8-10 leaves fresh sage
3 Tbl. olive oil
salt and pepper

Take the roast out of the refrigerator about an hour before placing it in the oven. Chop together well the garlic, rosemary, sage and thyme and rub the mixture over the entire roast. Salt and pepper all sides pressing the herbs and spices into the surface of the meat. Drizzle with olive oil. Place the roast in a baking dish or baking dish with a rack and insert a thermometer so that the tip is in the center of the roast.

Place uncovered, in a pre-heated 450° oven and immediately reduce the oven temperature to 350°. Bake until the thermometer reads 145-150° - approximately 1-hour - use the thermometer reading to determine when the roast is done, not the time. Pork tenderloin is likely to take less cooking time than a pork loin roast. When the roast has reached the desired temperature, remove from the oven, tent with aluminum foil, and let the roast "rest" for 10-15 minutes. This will keep the juices from running out when cut. Slice the roast and arrange attractively on a serving dish. Surrounding the sliced pork with sautéed, whole mushrooms would make a pretty presentation.

NOTE:

• Seasoning the roast with the garlic, herbs and pepper several hours or up to several days before cooking, and allowing it to "marinate" in the refrigerator covered with plastic wrap will deepen the herb flavors. Don't add the salt sooner than 1-hour before putting the roast in the oven.

• Use the tip of a small knife and stab the roast to make about a 1" deep gash. Push a garlic clove into the gash. Repeat in 7-8 other places on the roast so the garlic cloves are more or less evenly distributed.

• Pork tenderloin can be grilled instead of roasted. Follow instructions above but instead of placing the tenderloins in a baking dish, place on a medium, pre-heated grill. Imagine the tenderloins being three-sided and grill for 6-minutes per side. Remove from the grill, tent with aluminum foil to "rest" for about 10 minutes, slice, then serve.

Scallopini

Scallopini (or scaloppine) refers to a style of cooking where tender cuts of meat are pounded into small, thin cutlets, dredged in flour and finished with a winey sauce. This is a common cooking technique of Northern Italy that is seen in one variation or another, in many recipes from my Dad's side of the family.

Veal scallopini are the most classic of scallopini however, pork or chicken yield equally delicious scallopini. Because scallopini are cooked rather quickly, use the tenderloin cuts if using pork or veal, and the breasts if using chicken.

	1½ lb. veal
OR	1½ lb. pork tenderloin
OR	1½ lb. skinless boneless chicken breasts
	½ c. flour
	1 tsp. each dried thyme and rosemary
	½ c. oil for frying - ¼ c. vegetable oil and ¼ c. olive oil
	1 c. dry white wine or marsala
	3 Tbl. unsalted butter, cut into pieces
	salt and pepper

Cut the meat into slices about ⅓" thick and pound slightly to a thickness of about ¼" then cut the pounded cutlets into pieces about 1" x 2". Sprinkle the thyme and rosemary over the meat, and salt and pepper to taste. Put the flour on a plate and coat the meat with the flour shaking off any excess.

Heat the oil in a frying pan and cook the scallopini in batches tuning once so they are browned on both sides - be careful not to overcook otherwise they will be tough - at this point, it's okay if the meat is not cooked through. Drain on paper towels.

Discard the oil, reserving about 1 tablespoon. Place the pan on medium-high heat and return the scallopini to the pan. Add the wine/marsala and gently stir. Simmer slowly until the sauce thickens and scallopini are cooked through, about 3-5 minutes. (The flour on the scallopini will thicken the sauce as they cook together). Off heat, add the butter, mix until melted, and adjust the salt and pepper.

Serve over angel hair pasta or with risotto.

For Chicken Picante:
Follow the recipe above using chicken breasts. Do not cut the pounded cutlets - leave them in larger pieces. In addition to the wine, add the juice of 1 lemon, 1 teaspoon grated lemon rind, and 3 tablespoons capers. Serve topped with a squeeze of fresh lemon.

If you like mushrooms in your Chicken Scallopini or Chicken Picante, sauté some thinly sliced mushrooms in the reserved oil before returning the browned cutlets to the pan.

Serves 4-6

Rosemary Chicken

It would not be an understatement to say that our family dinners were feasts - the foods and meals providing the avenue for conversation, laughter and bonding. Feeding people is something that Italian women excel at and was proven time and time again by my nonne, mom and aunts in the abundance of antipasti, salads, pastas, polente and stews that graced their dinner tables. Among the many courses, inevitably a platter of aromatic and browned roasted meats where sure to be found. Chicken, sausage and pork were most common as was turkey on Thanksgiving. Sometimes we had veal, pheasant or rabbit, and on a few rare occasions had kid (capretto) or small birds. One Easter when I was a youngster, my Nonna Crocco roasted a whole kid. When I saw the beautifully cooked roast come out of the oven - its form obviously that of an animal - I had an epiphany of what farming and raising farm animals was all about.

Rosemary chicken is easy to prepare and is not only full of deep complex flavors but also looks beautiful heaped up on a serving platter. The aromatic woodsiness of the rosemary will fill your kitchen and tantalize your family and guests as the chickens roast.

This recipe takes advantage of the whole chicken however, selected cuts can be used instead. If using breasts, use bone-in, skin-on cuts to retain moisture and flavor.

> 2 whole chickens cleaned and cut-up
> 4 large springs fresh rosemary
> 2 cloves garlic, chopped fine
> 4 Tbl. olive oil
> 1 c. dry white wine
> salt and pepper

Arrange the chicken pieces on a large baking pan in a single layer (don't crowd the chicken or else they will not brown nicely, use two pans if necessary). Pull the rosemary leaves off of the stems and chop. Rub the rosemary, garlic, and salt and pepper on all sides of the chicken and then drizzle with olive oil. Be sure the skin-side of the chicken pieces are facing up.

Place the chicken uncovered in a pre-heated 400° oven and roast for 35 minutes until starting to brown. Pour the white wine over the chicken and roast for 15 minutes more. Remove from the oven and let stand for about 10 minutes. Baste the chicken with the pan drippings and serve. If desired, deglaze the pan drippings with a bit of white wine and serve on the side. The drippings can be reduced and/or fortified with butter or heavy/whipping cream if desired.

Serves about 10

Roasted Sausage with Potatoes

Fresh Italian sausage is classic in Italian cuisine which is why Italian grocers typically offer fresh sausage made on premise by one of their skilled and seasoned butchers. There were several such Italian markets in Detroit that my family frequented. Having accompanied my mom, Nonna and aunts on many, many shopping trips to these markets, the one I remember most vividly is Gonnella's - located on Oakwood Blvd. just a few blocks from my Nonna Zilioli's house. Among the hanging dried salami, rows of cold cuts and cheeses, and piles of fresh meats, Gonnella's showcased beautifully crafted fresh sausage mounded on trays in the butcher counter - each hand made and tied together with butcher string. Behind the counter stood a robust butcher weighing and wrapping his wares while bantering in Italian with the shoppers, most of whom he knew by name. I still buy my Italian sausage from a small, family owned Italian market in Phoenix, AZ. And although not Gonnella's, it conjures up memories of a little girl grocery shopping with her mom and Nonna every time I walk in.

Italian sausage is most commonly found in sauces, stews and stuffings, but as in this recipe, capably stands alone as a main course. Seek out an Italian grocer for good quality sausage which is likely to come in several varieties. My favorite is hot Italian sausage with fennel - but try them all to find yours.

2½ lbs. fresh Italian sausage
3 medium Russet potatoes
2 Tbl. olive oil
salt and pepper

Peel the potatoes and cut each one lengthwise into 6 wedges. Toss with the olive oil, and salt and pepper to taste. Arrange the potatoes and sausage in a large, oiled baking pan, more or less in a single layer. Bake at 375° for 60-70 minutes, carefully turning the sausage and potatoes several times to brown on all sides. If the potatoes need to brown a bit more, remove the sausage and place the potatoes in the broiler for about 5 minutes or until nicely browned. In any case, remove from the baking pan with a slotted spoon to drain off any excess drippings, and arrange the sausage and potatoes on a serving dish.

Serves 6-8

NOTE: Italian sausage can also be gently boiled in about 1" of water and browned once the water has evaporated, then served with boiled potatoes and/or cheese. Or, can be grilled and are delicious served in Italian buns with grilled bell peppers and onions.

Uccelli Scappat

My Dad's family is from Bergamo, a town in the Lombardy region of Italy, where roasted small birds are a popular and favored dish. Sometimes the hunters would return with a catch that was not sufficient for an entire meal so cooks, like my Nonna Zilioli, prepared small, meat packages stuffed with the same herbs they stuffed in the birds. They called them uccelli scappat (pronouned EWH-kah-lee ska-PAHT) - "birds that got away".

In Lombardy, small birds were usually roasted but because my Nonna didn't have an oven, she roasted them in a heavy skillet over a wood fire or as she did in Detroit, on top of the stove. Uccelli Scappat encompasses all of the typical flavors and cooking methods of Northern Italy so of course should be served with polenta.

2½ lbs. veal loin roast, cut and pounded into 8 cutlets
8 slices pancetta, sliced thin
3-4 springs fresh rosemary
16 leaves fresh sage
½ c. all purpose flour
4 Tbl. unsalted butter
1½ c. dry white wine
salt and pepper

Lightly salt and pepper both sides of a cutlet. Place a slice of pancetta in the center and lay two sage leaves and several rosemary leaves on top. Roll the cutlet, tucking in the sides and secure with toothpicks or tie with string (Nonna used string). Prepare the remaining cutlets in the same manner.

Coat the cutlets with flour shaking off the excess, and set aside. Melt the butter in a large, heavy sauté pan until it starts to foam but does not smoke or get too dark. Do not use a non-stick pan which prevents the meat from browning properly. The browning of the meat and butter is a key component to this dish's flavor. Place the cutlets in the hot butter and brown nicely on all sides.

Pour the wine over the uccelli scappat, cover and simmer for about 12-minutes until the sauce is slightly thickened, turn the uccelli scappat several times. Remove from the pan and set on a plate. Raise the heat and reduce the sauce to about half. Adjust the salt and pepper if needed. Serve the sauce and "small birds" on top of a freshly cooked polenta.

NOTE: Uccelli scappat is typically made from veal however, pork or chicken cutlets can also be used. I suppose if chicken is used the birds didn't really get away after all....

Vegetables

Asparagus with Eggs and Brown Butter

Asparagus with eggs and brown butter is the most delicious preparation of asparagus that I have ever eaten. It is a fabulous side-dish but also makes a wonderful light lunch or dinner.

If you select fresh asparagus that are about as big around as your ring finger, they will have more flavor than those that are small, pencil-sized. To remove the tough ends, hold each end of the stalk and bend. The stalk will naturally snap at the point where the asparagus begins to toughen.

2 bunches fresh asparagus
4 hard cooked eggs, peeled
6 Tbls. butter
6-7 fresh sage leaves
2-3 cloves garlic
⅓ c. grated parmesan cheese
salt and pepper

Wash and clean the asparagus, and remove the tough ends. Stream them for about 4 minutes until just tender - be careful not to overcook. While the asparagus are cooking, peel the garlic and slice into very thin lengthwise slices. Place the sliced garlic, sage leaves and butter in a small pan and place on medium low. Continue heating the butter, garlic and sage until the butter has a distinct nutty brown color and the garlic are toasty - about 5-7 minutes - don't let the butter smoke or burn.

Arrange the asparagus on a dish or platter. Slice the hard cooked eggs over the asparagus and top with the brown butter, garlic and sage. Salt and pepper to taste and then sprinkle with the parmesan cheese. Mmmmm.

To make perfect hard cooked eggs:
Place the eggs in a small pan and cover with at least 1" of cold water. Place on medium-high heat until the water comes to a full boil. Remove from heat, cover and let the eggs sit in the hot water for 27-minutes. Drain and cool the eggs by running under cold water.

Green Beans and Potatoes

This is one of my favorites. Although it is generally served as a side dish, I could easily have this as a main course. My Nonna Crocco grew Italian green beans in her backyard garden so each summer there was always an abundance of green beans for this dish. The Italian green bean has a much larger, flatter pod than the more common pole bean, however both varieties are equally delicious prepared as follows:

> 2 lbs. fresh green beans
> 4 medium russet potatoes
> 4-5 cloves garlic, peeled and smashed
> ¼ c. olive oil
> salt and pepper

Clean and snap the beans. If the beans are very long, cut them into about 3" pieces. Peel the potatoes and cut lengthwise into fourths and then crosswise into about 1" pieces. Place the potatoes first then the beans in a pot with 2" of water and simmer while covered until the beans are tender and the potatoes cooked through, about 12 minutes.

Drain off the water, and add the garlic and olive oil. Using a wooden or large spoon, mix well while mashing some of the potatoes with the back of the spoon. Some chucks of potato should be retained. Salt and pepper to taste.

6-8 servings

Broccoli

Broccoli is a pretty - not to mention flavorful and nutritious - vegetable that adds a touch of elegance to any table or plate where it is served. However, there is a dilemma that must be overcome when cooking broccoli in that, a single broccoli stalk requires two different cooking times. Cook it so that the flowers are still succulent, and the stalks will be too tough. Cook the stalks through, and the flowers end up as tasteless mush.

One might cook the flowers and stalks separately but then the attractiveness of the bright green broccoli stalk is lost. To overcome this problem, my Nonna Crocco devised a cooking method for boiling the stalks while simultaneously steaming the flowers. The result - perfect broccoli.

2 lbs. fresh broccoli
4 cloves fresh garlic
¼ c. olive oil
salt and pepper

Wash the broccoli and cut the bottom ¼" from the end of each stalk. Using a paring knife, peel the tough outer skin from the stalks beginning just below the flower clusters. Depending on the size of the stalk, cut each lengthwise into about 4 pieces keeping the flowers and stalk in tack with each piece. Arrange the stalks in a pot so that they are all "standing-up". In other words, so all the stalks are at the bottom of the pot and all the flowers are clustered together at the top. Use a pot that is just large enough to hold all the stalks so that they remain in their "standing" position. Add water to cover the stalks but not go beyond the point where the stalks begin to branch into the flower cluster. Cover, bring to a boil, and cook for about 5-7-minutes. Do not overcook the flowers.

While the broccoli is cooking, peel and slice the garlic into thin lengthwise slices. Place in a small pan with the olive oil and heat until the garlic are slightly brown. Drain the broccoli, arrange on a plater and pour the warm olive oil and garlic over the top being sure that some olive oil gets into each flower cluster. Salt and pepper to taste.

VARIATION: Put the garlic cloves in the water while the broccoli is cooking. To serve, break up the cooked cloves over the broccoli and then top with olive oil, salt and pepper.

Eggplant Parmesan

This is an elegant and mouthwatering dish that when served, will make any meal special and memorable. It is an absolute favorite of my brother, Larry, who in a quest for the perfect eggplant parmesan, has perfected the art of eggplant parmesan baking. He says, "eggplant parmesan is the single most compelling argument for becoming a vegetarian."

Many restaurants try to pawn off this dish as a few slices of fried eggplant covered with a ladling of tomato sauce and topped with cheese melted under a broiler. Perhaps tasty, it should not be confused with a classic eggplant parmesan which instead, is a layered casserole of infused flavors and textures that holds its own on a plate as a dense, savory cake of deliciousness. Served with a side of pasta, eggplant parmesan is a perfect meal.

One mistake often made when preparing eggplant parmesan, is using too much sauce and cheese so that when cut, the layers of eggplant slide off of each other making an unsightly mess. The perfect eggplant parmesan should have just enough sauce to be soaked up by the eggplant's bread crumb coating, and just enough cheese to add a creamy richness. A bit labor intensive, this is worth every minute.

> 3 medium eggplant
> 3 eggs
> 6-8 c. seasoned Italian bread crumbs
> 3½ c. sauce (see below)
> 1 c. grated Parmigiano-Reggiano cheese
> 2 c. shredded mozzarella cheese
> 2 c. vegetable oil or combination of vegetable and olive oil
> salt to taste

Cut the ends off of the eggplant and cut crosswise into ¼-½" slices. Break the eggs into a bowl, season lightly with salt and pepper, and mix until well blended; pour the bread crumbs on a plate. Dip an eggplant slice into the egg mixture, allow excess to drip off, and place in the bread crumbs. Coat completely pressing the bread crumbs firmly onto the eggplant, shake off excess crumbs and then place the eggplant on a wire rack. Continue until all the eggplant slices are breaded.

Heat the oil in a sauté pan until hot but not smoking, about 325-350°. Fry in batches - place a few of the eggplant slices in the hot oil so they are not crowded and cook until golden brown. Turn, and brown the opposite side - about 2 minutes per side. Remove from the oil and drain on paper towels, salt immediately.

Spread the bottom of a rectangular baking dish with ½ cup of the sauce and arrange a single layer of the fried eggplant slices over the sauce. Top the eggplant with 1 c. of sauce and ⅓ of each of the cheeses. Repeat two more times with eggplant, sauce, and cheeses until you have made three layers total.

Tent with aluminum foil and bake at 350° for 30 minutes, remove foil and bake 10 minutes more so cheese is just beginning to brown. Remove from the oven and let sit for 10-15 minutes. Cut into about 3" squares and serve with a side of pasta if desired.

<u>To make the sauce:</u>

> 1 medium onion, chopped
> 2 cloves garlic, chopped
> 3 Tbl. olive oil
> 2 15 oz. cans tomato sauce
> 1 6 oz. can tomato paste
> 2 Tbl. oregano
> 1 tsp thyme
> salt and pepper

Sauté the onion and garlic in the olive oil until the onions are soft and translucent, about 5-7 minutes. Add the tomato sauce, tomato paste, oregano, thyme and salt and pepper to taste. Stir to mix all ingredients then cover and simmer for 30-40 minutes stirring occasionally. To ensure the right texture and cohesiveness of the fully baked, sliced eggplant parmesan, this sauce needs to be thick – nearly the consistency of tomato paste. If needed, simmer uncovered until the right consistency is reached.

VARIATIONS:

- For a less pronounced eggplant flavor, peel the eggplant before slicing
- Slice the eggplant lengthwise
- Make the eggplant slices half as thick and make twice as many layers using half as much sauce and cheese on each layer. You may need more egg and breadcrumbs for the additional eggplant slices
- Replace the eggplant with 10-12 zucchini, cutting the zucchini either lengthwise or at a very steep bias.
- Replace the eggplant with a combination of eggplant and zucchini
- Although not quite as tasty, instead of frying, drizzle olive oil on the breaded eggplant and bake on a baking sheet in a 350° oven for 10-12 minutes.
- Sauté the eggplant slices in olive oil then use bread crumbs in the layers with the sauce and cheese.
- Some people believe the eggplant slices should be heavily salted on both sides and allowed to stand for 30 minutes to draw out excessive water before breading and frying. After a few minutes, the slices will "well up" with water droplets. If you choose to include this step, each slice should be rinsed with cold water and patted dry before breading and frying.

Fried Zucchini with Tomatoes

Garden freshness and simplicity makes this a delicious and satisfying meal. Our backyard gardens could be counted on to offer up baskets of zucchini and vine ripened tomatoes so during the summer, the ingredients for this dish were always in abundance. We piled the fried zucchini and tomatoes onto my Nonna Crocco's homemade bread for a succulent dinner sandwich.

This is perfect for larger zucchini that are about 10-12" long and 3-4" in diameter. However, several smaller ones can also be used.

> 1 large zucchini or 4-5 small
> 2 large ripe tomatoes, sliced
> 2 eggs
> 1½ c. seasoned Italian bread crumbs
> 8 slices homemade or good quality country style bread
> oil for frying
> salt

Cut the zucchini crosswise into about ⅜" slices. (If using smaller zucchini, cut on a steep bias). Beat the eggs in a shallow dish and place the bread crumbs on a large plate. Dip the zucchini into the eggs, lift and let the excess drip off.

Place the egged zucchini into the breadcrumbs and coat thoroughly by lightly pressing the breadcrumbs onto the zucchini. Set aside on a rack and continue unto all zucchini slices are breaded.

Heat 1" of cooking oil in a sauté pan to 325-350°. Place several zucchini slices in the oil, being careful they are not crowded. Cook for 1-2 minutes or until browned and then turn and brown the other side. Remove from oil and place on paper towels, salt immediately. Cook the remaining zucchini in the same manner.

Place several slices of the cooked zucchini on a slice of bread and top with tomato - salt the tomato if desired. Cover with another slice of bread, cut in half, and serve immediately. Any remaining zucchini slices can be served on the side.

Makes four sandwiches

NOTE: For a classic Italian flavor, cook the zucchini in one part olive oil and two parts vegetable oil.

Fritti

Although many types of vegetables can be prepared as fritti, in my family, fritti are either mushrooms or par-boiled cauliflower that are lightly battered and fried. Cardoona or burdock, a large, celery-like vegetable, is a popular fritti in Sicily; in other parts of Italy, it is common to find zucchini and artichoke heart fritti. Fritti, which means fried, refers to the cooking method rather than the thing that is cooked, so try a variety of vegetables for fritti misti (mixed), or stick with your favorite. Especially when fried in olive oil, fritti is a tasty vegetable dish that adds a little pizzazz to any meal.

<blockquote>
4 c. cleaned fresh mushroom
OR   4 c. par-boiled cauliflower flowerets
1 c. all purpose flour
2 egg
½ c. cold water
1½ c. oil for frying
salt
</blockquote>

Beat the eggs in a large mixing bowl until thoroughly blended; add the water, flour and 1 tsp. salt. Mix quickly into a batter being careful not to over mix. The batter should be the consistency of thin pancake batter so add a little more water or flour if needed.

Heat the oil in a frying pan until hot but not smoking about 325-350°. (If you use a 2:1 ratio of vegetable oil to olive oil, you can avoid the low-temperature smoking point of the olive oil while still imparting its delicious flavor). Making sure the vegetables are dry, place them in the bowl with the batter and stir gently until the vegetables are coated completely with batter. Lift the vegetables out of the batter, one piece at a time, let the excess batter drip off, and place into the hot oil. There should be ½-1" space between pieces. Cook for several minutes, turning if necessary, until batter is lightly browned and crispy all over. Remove from the oil and drain on paper towels; salt immediately. Continue frying the remaining vegetables.

NOTE: You can replace this batter recipe with other recipes for frying batters. Many modern batter recipes call for beer or soda water as the liquid ingredient. Additionally, several tablespoons of the flour are sometimes substituted with corn starch.   With the popularization of ethnic cuisines, pre-packaged tempura batter mix is readily available and is a good substitute as well.

Melanzana da Falerna

Melanzana, or eggplant in English, were commonly found in the vegetable gardens that my mom's family grew in Falerna, Calabria. It was no surprise, that when they moved to the US, baskets of this tasty and versatile vegetable were regularly harvested from their backyard garden in Detroit, Michigan.

In both Falerna and Detroit, during the summer when gardens flourish, melanzana were often simmered together with other garden produce. To preserve melanzana for the winter, my mom's family cut the melanzana into lengthwise slices and dehydrated them in the warm, dry Mediterranean sun. Once summer waned and the the garden's bounty dwindled away, they reconstituted the preserved melanzana by soaking the slices in water. My mom recollects, as one would expect, that they were not as good as fresh melanzana but a welcomed addition to a winter's meal.

This particular preparation of melanzana is somewhat stew-like with the other ingredients adding complexity to the taste and texture. We usually ate this with my Nonna's homemade bread, using it to soak up all of the flavorful juices from our plates.

	1 medium eggplant
	1 medium onion
	1 bell pepper
	2 cloves garlic
	1 large potato
	3 Tbl. olive oil
	1 28 oz. can whole stewed tomatoes
OR	2-3 fresh tomatoes cut in chunks
	1 Tbl. oregano
	salt and pepper

Clean and slice the onion and bell pepper into about ¼" slices; peel and chop the garlic. Peel the potato; cut in half lengthwise and then slice crosswise into thin slices. Sauté the onion, pepper and garlic in the olive oil for about 2- minutes. Add the potatoes and continue cooking for a couple more minutes.

In the meantime, julienne the eggplant into pieces about ¼-½" square and 3-4" long. Add to the pan, salt and pepper to taste, then mix with the other vegetables. Sauté for about 5 minutes, stirring occasionally until vegetable begin to limp. (You may need to add a bit more oil).

Remove the tomatoes from the can and cut into pieces adding the pieces and liquid to the vegetables. Season with the oregano and adjust the salt and pepper. Cover and simmer for about 15-20 minutes, stirring occasionally, so that the vegetables are tender. Serve with homemade or Italian bread to soak up all the juices.

OPTIONAL: For a more hearty meal, once the vegetables are cooked, make four "wells" in the simmering sauce by moving the vegetables aside with a wooden spoon. Break an egg into each well and cover to poach the eggs for about 3-4 minutes. Divide into four servings carefully spooning one of the eggs with each. This is how my Uncle Frank (aka Aki) likes this dish.

Melanzana Piccolo

If you think you don't like eggplant, you must try this dish. You will never think of eggplant in the same way after having these scrumptiously delicious Melanzana Piccolo - a savory eggplant mixture shaped into "little eggplant".

Eggplant were grown in abundance in our family gardens both in Italy and Detroit. These gorgeous, dark, shining globes are cooked in may tasty ways however, this eggplant dish is without a doubt my favorite. In my mind's eye, I can see my Nonna Crocco in her basement kitchen cooking this meal. If the eggplant were small, she cut them in half lengthwise, scooped out the flesh and then stuffed the eggplant shell with the savory eggplant mixture.

Melazana Piccolo freeze beautifully so that the summer eggplant harvest can be enjoyed during the winter months too. Yum, yum.

> 2 medium eggplant
> 1 c. dried bread crumbs
> ¾ c. crated parmesan cheese
> 3 eggs
> 4-5 cloves garlic mashed
> ½ c. chopped fresh parsley
> 1 tsp. each salt and pepper
> ½ c. oil for frying - half vegetable oil and half olive oil
> 4 c. tomato sauce - recipe below

Wash the eggplant and cut off the ends. Cut lengthwise into fourths; place into a pot with enough water to just cover the eggplant. Boil the eggplant until cooked through for about 8-10 minutes. Drain in a colander and allow to cool until they can be handled. When cooled, use your hands to tightly squeeze the water out of the eggplant. Place the eggplant on a cutting board and chop finely with a large knife so the eggplant is the consistency of ground meat. Place the chopped eggplant in a large mixing bowl and add the bread crumbs, ½ c. of the parmesan cheese, eggs, garlic, parsley, and salt and pepper. Mix so that all ingredients are well blended.

Using about ⅓ cup of eggplant mixture at a time, shape into ovals - they should more or less resemble the shape of a small eggplant. Heat the oil in a frying pan and fry the "little eggplants" in batches so that they are lightly browned on all sides. Remove from the pan and arrange in a single layer in a baking pan to which about ⅔ c. tomato sauce has been spread on the bottom. Cover the eggplant with the remaining sauce and top with the ¼ c. parmesan cheese. Cover the baking pan with aluminum foil and bake at 350° for 40-minutes. Remove the aluminum foil and bake 10-minutes more. Let the Melanzana Piccolo sit for 5-10 minutes before serving. Crusty Italian bread or cooked pasta make excellent accompaniments.

To make the sauce:

> 1 medium onion, chopped
> 2 cloves garlic, chopped
> 3 Tbl. olive oil
> 1 28 oz. can whole tomatoes
> 2 8 oz. cans tomato sauce
> 3 Tbl. oregano
> 2 tsp thyme
> salt and pepper

Saute the onion and garlic in the olive oil until the onions are soft and translucent, about 5 minutes. Run the whole tomatoes through a blender and add to the onion mixture along with the tomato sauce, oregano, thyme and salt and pepper to taste. Stir to mix all ingredients then cover and simmer for 30-40 minutes stirring occasionally.

Peas and Garlic

This is a quick, easy way to prepare peas. The result is bright flavor and color with just a hint of toothsomeness - a completely different experience than eating those drab green blobs in cans.

16 oz. fresh shelled or frozen peas
2 cloves fresh chopped garlic
3 Tbl. olive oil
salt and pepper

Heat the olive oil and garlic in a skillet on medium and then add the peas. Stir to coat the peas with olive oil then cover. Stirring frequently, cook for 3-5 minutes until peas are just cooked. Place in a serving bowl and salt and pepper to taste.

Potatoes with Cheese

Its obvious from its simplicity that this dish was born from a perspective of "here's all we have", rather than the cumulative inspiration from generations of cooks. Despite its seemingly pedestrian qualities, when we were kids we loved eating potatoes with cheese and thought of it as a treat because in addition to tasting surprisingly good, was very fun to eat. Taking a bite out of a whole, boiled potato has a sort of primal, gut-feel that just seems right.

4 medium potatoes
½ lb. mild-medium cheese like munster, tuma or fontina
salt

Slice the cheese and arrange on a plate; set aside to come to room temperature. Wash the potatoes and boil whole until just fork tender. Drain and set on a towel until cool enough to handle. Peel the potatoes and place in a bowl.

To eat, hold a potato in your hand taking a bite from the potato, followed immediately by a bite of cheese. Salt the potato lightly before each bite if desired.

Sautéed Zucchini

This is a quick, easy way to prepare zucchini and really highlights their mild, sweet flavor.

> 4 small zucchini, about 2" in diameter
> 1 medium onion
> 2 cloves garlic
> 3 Tbls. olive oil
> 1 Tbl. oregano
> salt and pepper

Peel and dice the onion and garlic. Sauté the onion and garlic in a large frying pan with the olive oil for about 2-3 minutes or until onions just start to soften. Cut the ends off of the zucchini and cut lengthwise into fourths. Slice crosswise into ¼" slices and add to the onions and garlic. Season with the oregano, and salt and pepper to taste. Cook for about 7-10 more minutes stirring occasionally until zucchini are cooked but not mushy.

VARIATION: When the zucchini are about half-way cooked, add a small can of tomato sauce or diced tomatoes. Simmer until zucchini are cooked but not mushy.

Zucchini Stew

This stew is a tasty medley of nice and chunky vegetables. So, although the flavors are blended and meld together, each vegetable stands on its own and can be savored separately. The traditional recipe includes Italian sausage however, if omitted, is just as flavorful as a vegetarian dish.

1½ lbs. Italian sausage
3 Tbl. olive oil
1 onion, diced
3 cloves garlic, peeled and
     chopped
1 bell pepper
2 stalks celery
5 carrots
2 medium potatoes
1 large can diced tomatoes
4 small zucchini
⅓ c. fresh chopped parsley
2 Tbls. dried oregano
salt and pepper

Cut the sausage into 2-3" pieces and brown slightly in a dutch oven. In the meantime, remove the seeds and membrane from the bell pepper and cut into 1" square pieces; peel and slice the celery into 1" pieces; peel the carrots and cut crosswise into thirds (remove ends); slice the zucchini crosswise into 1½" pieces (remove ends); peel and cut the potatoes lengthwise into fourths and then crosswise in half.

When the sausage are browned, remove them to a plate and drain any excess fat from the dutch oven. Add the olive oil, onion and garlic, lightly salt and pepper, and cook until the onion is softened and transparent. Add the bell pepper and celery and cook for several more minutes. Return the sausage to the dutch oven and add the potatoes, carrots, canned tomatoes, oregano and salt and pepper to taste. Cover and cook for about 7 minutes or until the potatoes are tender but not cooked through. Add the zucchini and parsley, cover and simmer for about 10 more minutes until all the vegetables are cooked.

Serve hot in large bowls.

Makes about 6 servings

Verdura

Cooked greens - regardless of cuisine - are the quintessential rustic food of rural, farming people. Of course, in Detroit, we were no longer farmers but with large patches of swiss chard gracing our backyard gardens, we were able

to preserve the tradition of our farming roots by eating cooked greens. The rows of tall, dark, curly leaves were absolutely beautiful and provided a steady harvest of fresh greens.

My mom's family grew greens year around in Calabria, sometimes shaking off snow before they were picked for that day's dinner. Most greens are hearty, sturdy plants and were therefore able to withstand the mild Mediterranean winters. During a time of year when other vegetables were either dried or preserved, winter greens added welcomed freshness to their meals.

We regularly cooked our garden's swiss chard into this dish that we call, "verdura". Verdura can be made with any type of greens although the cooking time may vary depending on the variety selected. Verdura is absolutely delicious, and as it has been for centuries, a very satisfying meal.

1½ lb. Italian sausage
2 lbs. swiss chard
3 Tbl. olive oil
1 medium onion, chopped
3 cloves fresh garlic, chopped
1 Tbl. oregano
2 tsp. thyme
1 can cannellini or northern white beans
3 medium potatoes
3 c. water or chicken broth
1 tsp. crushed red pepper (optional)
salt and pepper

Cut the sausage into 2" pieces and brown in the bottom of a heavy dutch oven. Remove the sausage from the pan and discard any excess fat that was rendered. Add the onion, garlic, crushed red pepper if using, and olive oil; sauté until onion is just beginning to get tender, 2-3 minutes. Return the sausage to the pan, add the water or chicken broth, cover and braise for about 5-7 minutes.

Clean and wash the swiss chard then cut both the leaves and stems, crosswise into 1" pieces. Peel and cut the potatoes into bite sized pieces. Add the potatoes and greens to the pot; salt and pepper to taste. The greens will loose a great deal of volume as they cook down so the pot may seem overfilled at first - just keep pushing the greens into the hot liquid until they are totally wilted. Add the oregano and thyme, and simmer covered, stirring occasionally, until greens are nearly cooked, about 12 minutes. Drain the canning liquid from the beans and add to the greens. Stir and cook about 10 minutes more. Serve with homemade bread for a classic rustic finish.

Makes about 8-10 servings

VARIATIONS:

- For a vegetarian version, omit the sausage and use vegetable broth or water in place of chicken broth. Use some herbs like thyme, oregano and/or fresh parsley for added flavor.

- Replace the Italian sausage with either country pork ribs or pork spare ribs and braise them until the meat is tender, about 1-hour, then continue with recipe.
- Substitute other greens for the swiss chard keeping in mind that cooking time varies with the type of greens. Escarole probably cooks the fastest while kale takes longest. Some greens, like mustard greens, can be bitter. In those cases, blanch the greens for about 3-minutes in boiling water before adding to the verdura.
- Although not always thought of as a green, this dish can also be made with cabbage.

NOTE: Behind the pretty girl (who happens to be my mom) is a typical backyard patch of swiss chard.

Bread

Making Bread

When my mom lived in Italy, her family had the good fortune of being able to produce enough food to never go hungry. Among their abundance of vegetables, figs, sausages, olives, cheeses and wine, the true life's blood staple was bread. Sustenance centered around the availability of this single food which accompanied literally every meal. Many times it was the very basis of the meal itself for example, when eaten at breakfast soaked in a bowl of sweetened milk and coffee, or eaten as a mid-day snack with figs and nuts.

Because of its culinary prominence and importance, a significant amount of the family's energy was spent on ensuring a consistent supply of bread. Unlike modern home-based bread-making methods where a plethora of flours can be purchased at the local grocery or specialty store, then prepared with bread machines or in temperature controlled ovens, their bread making began as a labor of love - growing the wheat then nurturing it through every step - culminating with fresh steamy loaves emerging from a hot brick oven.

Not all families had a brick oven so had to buy bread from one of the town's bakers. But my mom's family had a brick oven and made their own bread. The oven was at her grandmother's house, located in the rear of an open, airy, stable-like area where the smoke and heat could escape. About every three weeks, my mom's mother (my Nonna Crocco) and Nonna's older sister, Maria, who lived at her parents' along with her two children, made the family's supply of bread.

Here's how it was done:

Wheat was planted in the very early spring in ground that had been plowed with an ox. My mom's grandfather, Giovanni Menniti, would then spread the seed by tossing it in a wide arcing motion from a bag he carried as he walked through the field. The wheat was weeded as needed and was watered only by the rain as there was no irrigation.

By June, the wheat turned a beautiful golden color signaling the time for harvest. Two to five workers equipped with sickles would cut the wheat and arrange it in 1 foot diameter bundles that they tied together using a stalk of wheat as a piece of thin rope. The bundles were gathered into groups of 5-6 and stacked vertically with the cut ends on the ground and left to dry for about a week.

To separate the wheat from the straw, they cleared a large, flat area. To minimize the amount of wheat that might be lost in the dirt and rocks, they coated this area with a mixture of cow droppings and water. When throughly dried, this provided a hard surface for gathering the wheat. The golden wheat bundles were carried to this area and spread across its surface. Two oxen with a large stone tied to the yoke between them, walked in circles dragging the stone. This separated the wheat from the straw and also removed the outer sheath. Relying on the steady Mediterranean breezes, the workers then used large wooden pitch forks to winnow the wheat by tossing it into the air - the lighter straw was blown aside while the precious wheat berries, being much heavier, fell onto the prepared surface where it could be easily gathered. This process had to be repeated several times a day over a period of several days in order to harvest all the wheat.

In later years, someone from a neighboring town would bring a *trebiatrice* - a combine type of machinery, to separate the wheat from the straw. The workers, placed the wheat bundles in the *trebiatrice* which sent the wheat berries down a large chute where the workers would package the wheat in large burlap sacks. They left the filled sacks in the field along with neat bales of straw deposited by the *trebiatrice* - both were collected afterwards.

Regardless of its harvesting method, the wheat was stored in large wooden bins with hinged lids. The bins were divided into several sections - one section held the wheat.

When it was time to make bread, one of the women would take about 25 kilos of wheat to the local mill to be ground into flour. (The miller was a really nice man named Santo who gave my mom and the other children lupine beans for treats). The miller would carry the wheat up 4-5 steps to a platform where he could dump the wheat into a hopper. From there, the wheat traveled through the electrically run mill and was ground into flour. At the end of its journey, it fell through a chute and into sacks. For payment, the miller kept a percentage of the flour.

Because the resulting flour contained all components of the wheat kernel, it was sifted prior to being made into bread in order to remove the bran. They had a set of variable gauge sifters that were large pans about 1½ feet in diameter with screen bottoms. Typically, the flour was sifted through two gauges to remove the most and second most coarse bran flakes. (The bran was fed to the pigs along with whatever else they were fed that day). The resulting flour was similar to commercial whole wheat flours.

Whenever bread was made, about ⅓ lb. of dough - the *levato* - was saved and stored in the cupboard in an uncovered, ceramic bowl to serve as the starter for the next batch of bread. The day before bread making day, the *levato* which by then had formed a thick "skin", was placed in a warm bowl of water to soften and dissolve. Gently mixing with one's fingers helped to hasten this along. The now softened and dissolved *levato*, was mixed with about 2 kilos of flour and water to make a thick batter and left to sit over night. This new mixture - the *levatina* - was the starter for the bread itself.

There were times when someone wanted to make bread but had no *levato* so would borrow one. Social norm dictated that the *levato* borrower should return a *levato* to the lender from the batch of bread they made with the lender's *levato*. However, the borrower did not always return the *levato*, leaving the lender without a *levato* and on bread making day turning them into a *levato* borrower too!

Bread dough was made in the house, on a wooden, trough-shaped table where flour, water, salt and the *levatina* were mixed and kneaded usually by both my Nonna and Zia Maria because of the size and volume. After kneading, the dough was covered with a dusting of flour and a clean sheet then left to proof for a couple hours. Once proofed, the dough was cut into about 1 kilo pieces and worked into a ball, then shaped into *frise* and *wastedda* - one small piece of dough was put aside for the *levato*. The *frise* were large donut shaped loaves; the *wastedda* were pizza-sized flat breads. In the same room as the dough kneading table, the loaves were then placed on a bed that had been covered with a clean sheet to undergo a second proofing.

One of the women prepared the brick oven by building a wood fire inside the oven and leaving it to burn for about an hour or until the bricks turned white hot. The embers and cinders were cleared from the oven by scraping them into a bucket under the oven door with a tool that resembled a hoe. The remaining ash was cleaned from the oven with a mop made from ferns. As many times as necessary, they dipped the mop into a bucket of water and then wiped the bricks clean.

The *wastedda* were the first to go into the oven to test the temperature. If the *wastedda* came out overly browned, the oven was too hot and was cooled down by more water moppings with the fern mop. Through experience, the women knew when the oven had reached just the right temperature. The uncooked loaves proofing on the bed in the house were transferred to the outdoor oven on a large wooden board that the women carried on their head. Using a peel, they filled the oven with the loaves of bread and then closed the oven with a large metal door where the loaves were left to bake for about 30-minutes.

When the fresh-baked loaves emerged from the oven, they were placed in a large basket. The fresh batch of bread had to last the family for about 3-weeks so to prevent the bread from spoiling or going stale, the frise were cut horizontally and put back into the now cooling oven overnight. This essentially toasted the frise resulting in a dry, crispy texture. In this form, the frise could be kept in a large wooden bread bin for several weeks.

As a girl, I remember my Nonna Crocco regularly baking bread and often making frise which we called "hard bread". As a treat, my mom would prepare us a piece of frise like this:

> 1 3-inch square piece of frise
> 1 fresh garlic clove, peeled
> 1-2 Tbl. extra virgin olive oil
> 1-2 Tbl. red wine vinegar
> salt

Lightly scrape the garlic clove across the top of the frise. Drizzle with the olive oil and vinegar, lightly sprinkle with salt, and let soak for a few minutes - some sections of the frise will be nice and crunchy, others soft and flavorful with the olive oil and vinegar. Yum!!!

Nonna's Bread

One of the clearest memories I have of my Nonna Crocco is of her baking bread. She was an early riser and would finish what would be a day's work for most people, by about 8:00 in the morning. Every week, one of those mornings was dedicated to baking bread - not just a couple loaves of bread but six, seven, eight loaves of bread often in various sizes and shapes - each one crowned with a beautifully rounded brown top.

Bread, or *pane*, was ever present since it was considered a mealtime staple, and these loaves accompanied nearly every one of the week's meals. We visited Nonna regularly and often, so many a loaf found their way back to our house where we savored Nonna's bread on sandwiches, for our morning toast, or ate with dinner.

Nonna usually made her bread in the basement where she mixed and kneaded pounds of dough on an enamel table and left it to proof in a large, plastic wash tub. She swore by Robin Hood flour (although she would settle for Gold Medal) which she bought in 25 pound sacks at the local grocery store. She always checked for damaged or torn sacks because if she found one, she was sure to convince the store manager to let her have it at a discount. Nonna generally baked her bread in batches - the oven door propped shut with a large notched stick to keep the otherwise cockeyed hanging door securely closed - the house enveloped with the aroma of baking bread - and Nonna's relentless dedication to caring for her family abounding.

As children, my sister and I sometimes spent the night before bread-baking-day with Nonna. We waited in anticipation the next morning for her to take her loaves out of the oven because we knew that soon afterwards, we would be enjoying thick, warm slices of Nonna's bread with butter melting into its ever so slightly golden deliciousness.

Nonna's bread was originally made from a minimalist recipe using only the most basic bread ingredients - flour, water, salt and yeast. She added the shortening after she had been in the US for some years. Olive oil or lard was not used in the the bread she made in Italy nor in her early American made loaves. Modern tastes and the ubiquity of baking ingredients would call for a more full-flavored bread so I have put an updated "peasant" loaf recipe side-by-side with Nonna's. Bread making is a soulful and rewarding culinary art, and regardless of what kind of bread I am making, I always think of my Nonna.

Nonna's	Nonna's Updated
9 cups all-purpose flour (approx.)	9 cups all-purpose flour (approx.)
½ c. Crisco	½ c. vegetable oil or soft butter
3 c. warm water	3 c. warm milk
2 Tbl. salt	2 Tbl. salt
1.8 oz. fresh yeast	3 packages active-dry yeast (¾ oz.)
½ c. warm water	½ c. warm water
1 tsp. sugar	1 tsp. sugar
	¼ c. honey

Mix the yeast and sugar in ½ cup warm water and set aside to proof, about 5-minutes. Place the 3 cups warm water/milk in a large bowl. When the yeast has proofed, add it to the bowl with about half of the flour. Mix vigorously with a large wooden spoon to start the gluten development[1]. Add the Crisco/oil and salt, (also add the honey if making the updated version). Continue adding flour about 1 cup at a time until the dough is too stiff to mix with the spoon. At this point, turn the dough onto a floured work surface and beginning kneading in the remaining flour or enough to form a soft, but not sticky dough.

Knead the dough for 7-10 minutes until the dough is smooth and elastic and "pushes back" as you knead. Pull the dough together in a ball and place in a greased bowl. Grease the top of the dough and cover with a clean kitchen towel. Set the bowl in a warm, draft free spot and let the dough proof until

---

[1] I found that letting the dough rest for about 15-minutes at this point promotes good gluten development however, it was not a step in my Nonna's bread making process.

double in bulk, about 1 hour (when ready, the dough will leave an indentation when poked with your finger).

Punch down the dough and shape into three loaves and place each in a greased pan. Standard bread pans will result in a classic shaped loaf however, you can also make round loaves baked in cake pans, or form into large baguette shaped loaves and bake on a baking pan. In any case, cover the loaves with the kitchen towel and proof a second time for about 30 minutes.

Place the loaves in a 375° oven for about 30-40 minutes or until nicely browned and sounds hollow when thumped. Remove from the oven and let the loaves cool for about 10-minutes, then remove from the pans and cool on racks. For a special treat, slice a loaf while still warm (but not hot) and slather with butter.

Makes 3 loaves.

NOTE: In the 1970's, when awareness of the health benefits of whole grains was gaining popularly, Nonna sometime made whole wheat bread by replacing all or some of the all purpose flour with whole wheat flour. Look for whole wheat bread flour since its higher gluten content will result in a lighter loaf. If you use 100% whole wheat bread flour, you might want to add a bit more honey.

Breadsticks

Crunchy breadsticks to dip into bowls of soup, pair with cheese and salami, or munch all by themselves could be found in abundance on our family table. We sometimes bought breadsticks at the Italian grocery store that came perfectly stacked in clear cellphone bags with red lettering that signified their Italian authenticity. They were good, but never quite compared to a fresh, homemade breadstick that had been shaped and baked with loving care by my mom, Nonna or one of my aunts.

Breadsticks can be made in many different shapes and sizes, flavored with herbs, or topped with a variety of seeds but our breadsticks were typically plain and about 8-9" long and not quite an inch in diameter. During the 1970's when "natural" and less conventional foods and flavors began gaining popularity, we incorporated those trends into our breadsticks and made them with whole-wheat flour, in different shapes, and rolled in seeds - do some experimenting of your own - or make a batch in 2-3 different shapes, rolled in a variety of seeds and toppings. Whatever style breadstick you decide to make remember, capturing both crunchiness and tenderness is the secret to a truly exquisite breadstick.

3 c. all purpose flour
1 package active dry yeast
½ c. warm water
1 tsp. sugar
1 c. warm milk
2 Tbl.oil or softened butter
1 Tbl. salt

Place the yeast and sugar in a cup with the warm water and allow to proof. In the meantime, put the warm milk in a large mixing bowl along with the butter and salt. Add one cup of the flour and the yeast mixture then stir vigorously with a wooden spoon to start the gluten formation. Cover with a kitchen towel and let set for about 10 minutes. Add the remaining flour, turn out on a counter and knead until the dough just barely "pushes back" - about 7 minutes. Shape the dough into a round ball and place in a slightly oiled bowl, cover with a kitchen towel and place in a warm place to proof for about an hour or until double in size.

Punch down the dough and separate into 24 pieces. Roll each piece into a breadstick and place on a greased or parchment lined baking sheet. Cover the breadsticks and briefly proof for about 10 minutes.

Place the breadsticks in a pre-heated 350° oven for 10 minutes - the breadsticks should be cooked and solid but not yet browned. Reduce the oven temperature to 300°. Remove the breadsticks from the baking sheet and place them directly on the oven rack and continue cooking for another 10-12 minutes then turn off the oven and leave them in for another 10-15 minutes or until crunchy. Remove from the oven and cool on cooling racks. Dip in extra virgin olive oil, eat with cheese, dunk in wine or eat in your favorite way.

Makes 2 dozen

Frise

Making frise is a way to preserve bread so it can be stored for several weeks without molding or becoming stale. It is made from basic bread dough but instead of being shaped into loaves, it is shaped into a large doughnut by rolling the dough into a long log and pinching the ends together. Once baked and cooled, the frise are cut in half horizontally and placed back into a warm oven until toasty and dry.

My mom's family baked bread only once every several weeks and without refrigerators or freezers to store the loaves, they baked frise and kept them in large covered bins in their kitchen. Frise is a dry, crunchy bread, similar in texture to a breadstick so was sometimes sprinkled with water before eating to soften slightly. Often it was broken into pieces, placed in a bowl and soaked with hot broth, warm milk or latte.

My mom sometimes made us a snack by rubbing a piece of frise with a fresh garlic glove then sprinkling with olive oil and red wine vinegar. The oil and vinegar would soften the frise while still leaving a nice crunch, and the pungent garlic added just the right amount of zing.

> 1 loaf's worth of bread dough
> 1 glove fresh garlic, peeled
> 2 tsp. olive oil
> 2-3 tsp. red wine vinegar

Roll the dough into a 2 foot log and shape into a doughnut by pinching the ends together. Place on a oiled or parchment lined baking sheet to proof for about 20-25 minutes, then bake at 375° for about 30-35 minutes or until golden brown.   When the frise is cooled, cut in half horizontally. My Nonna would make a small cut on one edge of the frise and then fit a piece of butcher string into the cut so that the string would wrap around the circumference of the frise.   Holding the ends of the string together, she worked the string through the frise is a seesaw motion until it was cut into two.   Although this is an interesting and cleaver method, a good bread knife will do.

Place the frise cut side up, in a 250° oven for about 2 hours until dry and crunchy.   When it's cool, break off a piece about the size of a slice of bread and rub with the fresh garlic glove then sprinkle with olive oil and red wine vinegar.   Let set for about 5-minutes before eating.   Delizioso.

Taralli

During the summer, my mom, her sister and their cousins would stay with their maternal-grandfather, Giovanni Menniti, at "la mare" (the ocean) to help tend one of the family's farming properties. Although they genuinely worked as farm hands, they also had fun being together and swimming in the Mediterranean Ocean every day.

La mare was several miles from the town where they lived and had to be traveled to by foot, making it impractical to go back and forth each day. Instead, the family just stayed there for several weeks at a time. Life at la mare was somewhat like camping with limited food preparation and storage amenities, so food-stuffs brought from home had to keep well on their own, for many days.

Taralli, a crunchy, donut-shaped breadstick with a long shelf-life were ideal. My grandmother and great-grandmother made taralli then packed them up for the trip to la mare knowing they would made a tasty snack or yummy breakfast when softened in warm latte.

1½ c. whole-wheat flour
1-1½ c. all-purpose flour
2 Tbl. extra virgin olive oil
¼ c. warm water
1 package dry-active yeast
1 c. dry white wine or water
1 Tbl. fennel seeds, crushed
1 tsp. salt

Mix the yeast in the ¼ c. warm water and set aside to proof. Warm the wine (or water if using) to slightly above room temperature and place in a mixing bowl with the olive oil, salt and crushed fennel seeds. Add the whole-wheat flour and yeast mixture and beat with a wooden spoon until well blended. Mix in the all-purpose flour about ½ cup at a time, until a smooth soft dough forms. Turn the dough onto a lightly floured counter and knead for 5-7 minutes then form into a ball, and place in an oiled bowl covered with a clean kitchen towel. Set aside to rise for 60-80 minutes or until not quite double in size.

When the dough is done rising, punch down and shape the taralli by pinching off a piece of dough about the size of a large walnut (1 oz.) and rolling it into a rope the thickness of your baby finger. Shape the rope into a circle by bringing the ends together crossing one end over the other. Push your index finger into the spot where they cross 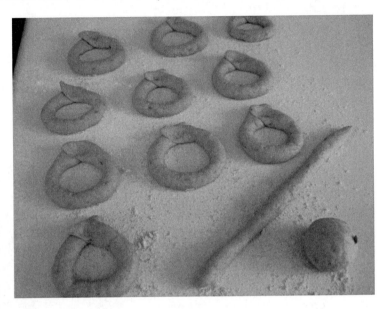 to secure the two ends. Set the taralli on a floured counter or sheets of parchment, cover and let rise until double in size - about 60-minutes.

Fill a wide-rimmed pan or pot with several inches of water and bring to a light boil. Working in batches, boil the taralli for about 20 seconds per side. Lift out of the water with a large slotted spoon and drain briefly on a kitchen towel (not terrycloth). Arrange the boiled taralli on parchment lined baking sheets and bake in a 350° oven for 25 minutes. Remove them from the baking sheets and lay them directly on the oven rack and bake for another 10 minutes. Lower the oven temperature to 250°, turn the tarralli over ,and leave them in the oven for another 20-30 minutes until crunchy.

Makes about 20

Cuddurieddi

Cuddurieddi (or cullurielli) - fluffy and warm, honey drenched morsels of fried potato dough - are traditionally made on Christmas Eve. In Falerna, where my mom grew-up, cookies, donuts and other desserts were not readily available and were essentially absent from the families' day-to-day culinary repertoire. Consequently, cuddurieddi where a rare and highly anticipated treat being one of the few, if not only, "sweets" that my mom and her family indulged in during the year. Sometimes the honey coated cuddurieddi were also sprinkled with sugar and a savory, anchovy stuffed variety were fried in the final batch. (The anchovy variety are cooked last because of a "fishy" taste they impart to the frying oil).

My Nonna Crocco made mounds of cuddurieddi usually on New Year's Day. Most everything she cooked she did on a grand scale and cuddurieddi were no exception, using as much as 10 pounds of potatoes and an equally enormous amount of flour. A single batch of raised dough rounded over the top of a 3-4 gallon plastic wash tub while a large roaster holding several quarts of cooking oil, sitting across two burners on her basement stove served as the cuddurieddi fryer.

Nonna, my mom and aunts, and us kids spent the afternoon in Nonna's basement frying batch after batch of cuddurieddi and rolling them while still hot, in bowls of golden honey. The men were usually watching football or playing poker so one of us would whisk heaping platters of still warm cuddurieddi upstairs for them to devour.

My brother, Larry, and our mom and dad continue with the cuddurieddi tradition on Christmas Eve by getting together for dinner and cuddurieddi making. They have even refined the preparation process (might have something to do with both my dad and brother being engineers) by oiling, instead of flouring, their hands and work surface whereby eliminating any excess flour that would otherwise burn and smoke in the cooking oil. None the less, as Christmas approaches, cuddurieddi are still a rare and highly anticipated treat.

6 large Idaho potatoes (about 3-lbs.)
7 c. all purpose flour
3 Tbl. yeast
3 tsp. salt
2 eggs
1½ c. warm (not hot) water
4 c. high quality cooking oil for frying
3 c. honey
½ c. sugar (optional)
6-10 anchovy fillets (optional)

Wash the potatoes, place in a large pot and cover with water. Bring to a boil and simmer for about 20-25 minutes or until the potatoes are fork tender. Drain the potatoes and when cool enough to handle, peel, mash and set aside to cool.

Stir the yeast into the water and allow to proof. In the meantime, mix the flour and potato in a large mixing bowl. Beat the eggs and add to the flour-potato along with the yeast mixture and salt; mix well. Knead the dough for about 5-6 minutes or until smooth adding more water or flour as needed to make a bread-like dough. Form into a round ball, cover with a clean kitchen towel and let proof for about 45-60 minutes until doubled in size.

Once the dough has doubled, heat the oil in a deep pan or dutch oven to about 325-350°. Lightly oil your hands to prevent sticking and without punching down the dough, cut the dough into strip-like pieces about 5" long and 1" square, gently pull lengthwise and lower into the hot oil (do not crowd the cuddurieddi). Cook until golden brown on all sides, about 2-3 minutes. Remove from the oil, drain slightly and while still warm, roll each cuddurieddi in the honey. Sprinkle with sugar if using.

For savory cuddurieddi - before frying the last batch, shape the cuddurieddi as for sweet then flatten slightly, place 1-2 anchovy fillets in the center, bring the long edges together and pinch shut. Fry as for sweet but omit honey and/or sugar.

Enjoy while still warm.

Makes about 4 dozen

Fried Dough

For lunch on Saturdays, Aunt Teresa often made fried dough served with cheese. Uncle Al was Bolognase and fried dough or crecentine as they are called in Bologna, was a dish that Aunt Teresa learned from his family. This unassuming meal of puffed and crispy bread with cheese makes a wonderful meal that for us was always a special treat.

Serve fried dough with your favorite semi-soft cheese - munster, fontina, tuma or similar cheese would be good choices. Or, enjoy them accompanied with cured meats as the Bolognase often do.

> 1 c. warm milk
> 3 c. all purpose flour
> 1 package active dry yeast
> ¼ c. warm water
> ½ tsp. sugar
> 2 Tbl. butter, softened
> 1 tsp. salt
> vegetable oil for frying

Mix the yeast, water and sugar in a small bowl or cup and allow to proof. In another mixing bowl, add the milk, butter and salt. Add 2 cups of the flour, the proofed yeast mixture and mix with a wooden spoon. Turn onto a well floured work surface and knead in the remaining flour to make a bread dough. Knead for 5-7 minutes then roll into a ball, place in a greased bowl and cover with a kitchen towel until double in bulk, about 1 hour.

Heat 2 inches of vegetable oil in a heavy skillet to about 350°. While the oil is heating, punch down the dough and roll it out into a ½ inch thick rectangle. Cut the rectangle into 4-5 inch strips and then cut the strips crosswise into rectangles. Carefully slide several rectangles into the hot oil and fry until browned and puffy. Flip, and brown the other side. Remove from oil and drain on paper towel, salting the fried dough while they are still hot. Fry the remaining rectangles until they are all cooked.

Serve while still warm with slices of cheese and have a great Saturday lunch.

Gudzupe

When we visited Nonna Crocco during Easter, instead of baskets filled with candy bunnies and foil wrapped chocolate eggs, she had a table full of whimsical and delicious gudzupe waiting for us. Gudzupe is a braided, yeast bread cradling still-in-the-shell eggs and were an icon of the family's Easter celebration in Calabria. Braided, ring-shaped breads adorned with eggs were made for the adults and the family meal. Smaller, single-egged loaves -meant to resemble fish - were made for the children.

In Calabria, the gudzupe were made from regular bread dough however, in the US over time, the dough became richer and sweeter. My Aunt Tina (who married my Uncle Frank, aka Aki) is Polish and we adopted her family's sweet bread recipe for our gudzupe. Nonna decorated her gudzupe with raw eggs that cook while the gudzupe bake but in more recent years, we have been first coloring the raw eggs which give the gudzupe a lovely springtime accent.

This is a rich dough so be sure to use the full amount of yeast, and allow a little extra time to proof. Gudzupe is delicious in its own right but when sliced and toasted is exceptional.

> 2½ c. warm milk
> 10 c. all purpose flour (approx)
> 4 eggs, beaten
> 2 sticks margarine, softened
> 1 Tbl. salt
> 3 Tbl. dry yeast
> 1½ c. sugar
> ½ c. warm water
> 10 eggs for decoration (color ahead of time)
> 1 egg for glaze
> 2-3 c. raisins (optional)

Place the warm milk, salt and 3 cups of the flour in a large mixing bowl and beat with a wooden spoon until mixture is sticky and starts to pull away from the sides of the bowl. Allow to sit for about 10 minutes (this promotes the gluten development which gives bread good structure). In the meantime, mix the yeast, water, and about ½ teaspoon of the sugar is a small bowl or cup and leave undisturbed until it becomes a little foamy. Add the yeast, eggs, sugar and another 2 cups of flour to the dough and mix. Add the margarine and raisins if using, then start working in the remaining flour to form a soft bread dough - it should be sticky at this point.

Turn the dough onto a floured work surface and knead in enough additional flour to form a soft dough. Continue kneading for for about 7 minutes - flour the work surface and your hands just enough to prevent sticking but be careful not to get the dough too stiff.

Form the dough into a ball, place in a greased bowl then cover the bowl with a kitchen towel and allow the dough to proof for about 75 minutes. Because this dough is so rich, it probably won't rise as much as a plain bread dough. Punch down the dough, form into a ball, and cut off not quite ½ of the dough. Cut into 3 equal pieces and roll each piece into a 2-2½ foot rope. Make a loose braid with the 3 ropes then pull the ends together to form a ring and weave the ends into each other to connect the ends. Place on a parchment lined baking sheet and place 6 colored eggs, pointy end down, in between the braids.

Cut the remaining dough into 4 equal pieces and roll each into about an 18 inch rope. Working with one rope at a time, bring the ends of the rope towards each other to form a U. Place a colored egg in the bend of the U and then crisscross the rope leaving about 1½ inches at the end. Flatten the ends and cut 3-4 slits in each end to resemble a fish's tail. Place on parchment lined baking sheets.

Cover the gudzupe and proof for 35 minutes. Brush the dough with a beaten egg and bake in a 325° oven for 30-40 minutes or until slightly browned and sounds hollow when thumped. Remove from the oven and cool on racks. The gudzupe are delicious with butter and makes a scrumptious breakfast when toasted.

NOTE:

This dough can be shaped into regular bread loaves or dinner rolls and enjoyed any time of the year as a delicious sweet bread. Aunt Tina's mom, Rose, used to make clover leaf rolls - three small balls of dough placed in a greased muffin tin. Sweet bread is very good with a light glaze made with powered sugar, milk and a touch of vanilla extract.

Pizza Piena

Breads flavored with lard can be found throughout southern Italy in celebration of spring and Easter. It is widely known among chefs and down-home cooks alike that using lard as the shortening in breads and pastries results in some of the tastiest and flakiest. Pizza Piena is definitely one such bread. It is wonderfully flavored, beautifully textured and is especially delicious warm or toasted.

6 c. all-purpose flour
2 packages active-dry yeast
2 c. warm water
½ c. melted lard
6 eggs
1¼ c. pepperoni or salami cubed (the size of small dice)
1½ c. mozzarella cheese cubed (the size of small dice)
2 tsp. salt

Hard cook 4 of the eggs, peel and slice. Mix the yeast in ½ cup of the warm water and set aside to proof. Slightly beat the remaining 2 eggs and place in a large mixing bowl with 1½ cups warm water, the melted lard and salt. Add 3 cups of the flour along with the yeast mixture and beat with a wooden spoon until well blended. Add the remaining flour 1 cup at a time, until a dough forms. Turn the dough out on a lightly floured counter and knead for 5-7 minutes until smooth and elastic - add more flour as needed to prevent sticking.

Flatten the dough to form a rectangle and evenly sprinkle the pepperoni or salami, cheese and sliced cooked eggs over the dough. Incorporate the meat-cheese-egg filling into the dough by gently rolling up and kneading. Shape into a ball and place in an oiled bowl covered with a clean kitchen towel until doubled in size - about 60 minutes.

Punch down the dough and cut it into two even pieces. Shape each piece into a loaf and place in oiled bread pans. Cover the pans with the kitchen towel and set aside to rise for 30-40 minutes until doubled in size.

Brush the top of the loaves with beaten egg or a little melted lard and bake in a pre-heated 375° oven for about 35-40 minutes until golden brown and sounding hollow when tapped.

Cool on racks and enjoy while still warm.

Pizza

There is a lot of hype around minimalist, thin-crusted pizzas beautifully charred from being baked for only a few minutes in red-hot, wood-burning brick ovens. But, this recipe is not one of those kinds of pizzas, nor does it try to be. Pizza is an Italian-American dish that my Nonna added to her culinary repertoire once in the United States and her's is a hearty pizza - nothing minimalist about it - with chewy, crunching crust covered with robust toppings busting with flavor. One or two slices is all it takes to make a meal - Nonna's pizza is definitely one of our favorites.

Perfect pizza has a crust that is neither too thin nor too thick, is browned and crunchy on the bottom yet chewy and soft to the bite. The toppings, regardless of what they are, should be of high quality with no single topping overpowering the others. The toppings should be generous but not so much so that the crust cannot stand-up to their weight. When you bite into a slice, the reaction should be mmmm-delizioso.

This is a tasty, all-around pizza but can be made with a host of different toppings. It makes a single, large pizza but can be multiplied by however many pizzas you are making.

> 1 crust
> ½-¾ c. pizza sauce
> ⅓ c. grated parmigiano reggiano
> 1 lb. grated mozzarella cheese
> 1 pepperoni stick, sliced thin (Margherita brand is best)
> 1 lb. hot Italian sausage, casing removed and sautéed
> 1 bell pepper, sliced
> 1 c. sautéed sliced, fresh mushrooms

Punch down the dough and roll out the crust to the size of your pizza pan (a screen bottomed pizza pan will bake good pizzas in a regular household oven). Brush the pizza pan with olive oil and lay the crust on the pan; pull and shape the edges as needed to conform to the pan. Go all around the edge of the pizza crust and push it in towards the center just enough to form a slight ridge. Cover and let rise for about 10 minutes.

Drain off any excess fat from sautéing the sausage. Brush the crust with olive oil and then top with the pizza sauce. Use the back of a spoon and spread the sauce evenly over the entire pizza including the ridge of dough at the edges. Sprinkle with the parmigiano reggiano, then top with the sausage, peppers and mushrooms. Cover with the mozzarella cheese then layer like shingles, with the pepperoni. Be sure that all the topping go all the way to the edge of the pizza so you end up with full (not partial) slices.

Place the pizza on the bottom rack of a 450° oven for about 15 minutes. Turn the pan so the front of the pizza is now at the back of the oven about half way through the cooking time. Each oven is a little different so watch the pizza closely and adjust the baking time to when the pizza is nicely browned and the bottom crust golden and crisp (you can peak at the crust by lifting an edge with a spatula). **NOTE:** If you are baking more than one pizza at a time, bake for 10 minutes, then switch the pizza on the bottom rack with the pizza on the rack above and bake 10 minutes more or until nice and brown on top and on bottom crust.

Remove from the oven, slide the pizza off the pan onto a cutting surface, and cut into 8 pieces with a large heavy knife or pizza cutter. Keep the slices on a cooling rack so air can circulate under the bottom crust, otherwise the steam from the hot pizza will make the crust soggy.

For a mediterranean twist replace the sausage, pepperoni, peppers and mushrooms with marinated artichoke hearts, thinly sliced red onion, and kalamata or other black olives.

To re-heat the pizza, place a slice(s) on a sheet of aluminum foil laid directly on the rack of a 350° oven for about 15 minutes. Do not use the microwave - it will significantly compromise the texture of the crust.

Enjoy.

<u>For the crust:</u>

3 c. bread flour
1c. warm water
3 Tbs. olive oil
2 tsp. salt
¼ c. warm water
1 package active dry yeast
½ tsp. sugar

Combine the ¼ cup warm water, yeast and sugar in a small bowl and set aside to proof, about 5 minutes. Mix the 1 cup warm water, olive oil and salt in a large bowl. Stir in half of the flour and proofed yeast mixture and beat with a wooden spoon until sticky and pulling away from the side of the bowl. Add the remaining flour and turn out on a floured work surface. Knead the dough for about 7-minutes or until it "pushes back". Roll into a ball and place in an oiled bowl. Cover with a kitchen towel and allow to proof until double in size, about 1-hour.

For the sauce:

1 7 oz. can tomato sauce
2 Tbs. olive oil
½ onion diced fine
2 cloves garlic chopped
4 tsp. dry oregano
salt and pepper to taste

In a small sauce pan, sauté the onions and garlic in the olive oil until the onions are soft but not brown. Add the tomato sauce, oregano, and salt and pepper. Mix well then cover and simmer on medium-low for about 20-25 minutes stirring occasionally. Remove from the heat and allow to cool slightly.

Cookies & Desserts

Apple Fritters

These fritters are extra delicious when warm and steamy. Apple fritters were one of the many fritters that my Nonna Zilioli often made. Her recipe had no cinnamon or nutmeg but I think it amps up the fritters with a more decadent flavor. Apple fritters are also wonderful for a special breakfast treat. Be sure to fry the fritters until well browned to ensure they are cooked through.

1⅓ c. sifted flour
3 Tbl. sugar
2 tsp. baking powder
½ tsp. salt
2 eggs
⅔ c. milk
1 Tbl. cooking oil
3 c. apples, peeled and sliced thin
oil for frying

Pour about 2″ of oil in a pan and heat on medium. While the oil is heating, use a large mixing bowl, and mix together the flour, sugar, baking powder and salt. In a separate bowl, whisk the eggs, milk and 1 Tbl. cooking oil. Pour the liquid mixture into the bowl with the dry ingredients and stir 4-5 times then add the apples and mix thoroughly using as few strokes as possible. Over mixing will cause the fritters to be tough, so stop stirring as soon as everything is incorporated.

When the oil reaches 325-350°, fry the fritters by dropping about ¼ c. of batter into the hot oil and flatten slightly taking care to not over crowd the fritters. When the edges are browned, flip the fritters and brown on the other side. Continue cooking the fritters for 2-3 more minutes, flipping a couple times so that the batter in the center of the fritter is cooked through. (You can remove one of the fritters from the oil and cut into the center to check if they are done.)

Lift the fritters from the oil and drain on paper towels. Dust generously on all sides with powdered sugar and place on a serving plate. Continue frying fritters until all the batter is cooked. Eat the fritters while warm with fresh hot coffee or a tall glass of milk.

Makes about 1½ dozen fritters

Biscotti

These are the best biscotti - they have perfect texture and just the right amount of sweetness. This is my mom's recipe and I make a double batch every Christmas. In addition to their scrumptiousness, biscotti store amazing well so once baked, can be enjoyed for weeks.

The base recipe is versatile and can be embellished to make many, many variations. I've included a few of my favorites but go ahead, and create some of your own!

> 2 sticks butter, softened
> 2 c. sugar
> 4 eggs
> 2 tsp. vanilla extract
> 4 c. flour
> 4 tsps. baking powder
> ½ tsp. salt
> 2-3 c. add-ins (depending on variation)

Cream together the butter and the sugar until fluffy. With mixer running, add the eggs one at a time until combined and then add the vanilla. In a separate bowl, mix the flour, baking powder and salt then combine with the butter-sugar-egg mixture. The consistency should be similar to pie crust so if needed, add a little flour if too sticky or water if too dry then stir in the add-ins

Divide the mixture into fourths and shape each into a log 1½-2" in diameter and about 8-10" long. Place two logs on each of 2 cookie sheets lined with parchment paper and bake in a 350° oven for 25-30 minutes. Be sure to switch racks and rotate pans half way through baking time. When slightly browned, remove from oven and cool on a rack or counter for about 15 minutes.

With a serrated knife, cut each log on the bias into slightly less than ½" slices. Arrange the slices on the cookie sheets and return to the oven to bake about 15-20 minutes more or until the biscotti are browned and crispy flipping them over half way through. Remove from the cookie sheets and cool. Repeat with remaining biscotti.

Makes approximately 4 dozen

VARIATIONS:

Almond-Anise
> 2 tsp. anise seeds
> 2 c. slivered almonds

Cherry-Chocolate
> 1½ c. dried cherries
> 1-1½ c. mini chocolate chips

Lemon-Poppy Seed
> replace vanilla extract with 2 Tbl. lemon extract
> grated rind of 1-2 lemons
> ½ c. poppy seeds

Orange-Chocolate
> replace 1 tsp. vanilla extract with grated rind of 1 orange
> 2 c. chopped walnuts

To finish the biscotti – melt 8 oz. of chopped semi-sweet chocolate in a double boiler. Use the back of a teaspoon and spread a small amount of melted chocolate on one side of each biscotti. Allow chocolate to set, about 2 hours.

Roasted Castagne (Chestnuts)

At the onset of fall when the days begin getting shorter and the landscape changes color, castagne appear as do autumn evenings filled with munching their roasted, sweet goodness. When we visited Nonna Zilioli during castagna season (Oct-Jan), along with coffee and biscotti, she served us freshly roasted castagne as they were customarily offered to guests in Bergamo. Nonno sat at the end of the dining room table (where he could see the TV) and used his pocket knife to cut a slit along the flat side of each castagna (a necessary step to prevent the castagne from exploding in the oven while roasting). Nonna would take the pan of castagne and roast them in the oven then carry the freshly roasted castagne from the kitchen wrapped in a damp kitchen towel that she unfolded at the dining room table releasing their warm, nutty aroma. We had many visits sharing a batch of warm, roasted castagne and I still see this image in my mind's eye every time I eat one.

1 lb. castagne (chestnuts)

Using the tip of a small, sharp knife, pierce the shell on the flat side of the castagna then cut about a ½" slit. Place the castagne on a baking sheet in a single layer and roast in a preheated 425° oven for 15-20 minutes.

Remove from the pan and cool just enough to handle. To loosen the shell, set a castagna on the table or counter and give it a gentle wrap with the palm of your hand. Peel away the shell and enjoy while warm.

NOTE:
Castagne have a golden-tan inner shell that should also be removed. Usually, it adheres to the outer shell during roasting and the two shells come off together. However, if after you peel the castagna you notice that some inner shell is still attached, just peel it off as it is slightly pubescent and not particularly tasty.

Makes about 2 cups peeled

Nonna's Fig Cookies

Nonna Crocco made these cookies but never really had a name for them except 'fig cookie'. I hadn't thought about these cookies for years until a Calabrase acquaintance of mine, Corrie, let me sample a similar cookie that had been given to her at Christmas time. She called them 'chichinelli' which was a totally unfamiliar word for me however, I immediately recognized the taste as soon as I took a bite.

Nonna was living in an assisted living facility at the time and hadn't made cookies for years but during one of my visits back to Detroit, I thought I would ask her about the fig cookies anyway. To my astonishment, Nonna immediately gave me her recipe of:

    7 lbs. of flour
    1½ lbs. sugar
    ½ lb. Crisco
    14 eggs
    6 tsp. baking powder

Nonna always cooked in giant portions so when I got back to Phoenix, I calculated her recipe to the proportion below. Amazingly, the recipe as Nonna recalled from memory was correct – I only added some water and lemon rind to round out the texture and flavor.

Like the cookie Corrie fed me, I have since seen (and eaten) variations shaped like pin-wheels or crescents however, Nonna always made them stuffed and shaped like ravioli. They are a delicious and festive looking cookie. My husband, Ray, says they remind him of Fig Newton – but much better of course!!!!

Filling

    ½ lb. dried figs
    3 oz. dried dates
    2 oz. raisins
    Rind and juice from ½ lemon
    2 c. water

Pastry

    4 c. flour
    ⅓ c. sugar
    1 Tbl. grated lemon rind
    ¾ c. butter or Crisco
    2 eggs
    2 tsp. baking powder
    ½ tsp. salt
    ½ c. water, approximately

Glaze

    1 c. powdered sugar
    1 tsp. grated lemon rind
    3-5 Tbl. fresh lemon juice
    Colored nonpareils for decoration

To make the filling, remove the stems from the figs and the pits from the dates. Coarsely chop and place them in a heavy pot with the raisins and water. Cook for about 20 minutes on medium-low heat until the fruit is soft and moist. Add a little more water if needed. Remove from heat and cool slightly. Working in batches, whirl the cooked fruit in a food processor just enough to form a uniform filling. Add the lemon rind and lemon juice and mix well.

For the pastry, mix together the flour, sugar, baking powder, salt and lemon rind. Cut in the butter or Crisco as you would for pie crust. Mix together the eggs and water and blend into the flour mixture to form a soft, but not sticky, dough.   Add a little more flour or water if needed to achieve the right consistency.   Knead slightly, just until dough forms into a ball and chill for about 10-minutes.

To assemble the cookies, roll out about a fourth of the pastry into a ¼" thick rectangle. Starting at the top of the rectangle, place rounded teaspoons of the filling in a straight line, an inch apart and about 2 inches from the edge. Take the top edge of the pastry and fold it over the dollops of filling. Seal the edge by pressing the dough together with your finger tips.   Now, starting at the center, seal the sides of the cookies by pressing your index finger between the dollops to seal. Continue towards both ends and push the air out as you work. Make sure all the edges are sealed. Cut the row of cookies away from the sheet of pastry and then separate the individual cookies by cutting in between. Seal the cut edges with the tines of a fork and place the cookies 1½" apart on a parchment lined cookie sheet. Poke the top of each cookie with a fork so steam can escape while baking. Repeat process with remaining rolled dough. Roll out the rest of the dough, a forth at a time, and continue as described above.   Bake the cookies at 375° for 25-30 minutes until lightly browned. Remove cookies from the cookie sheet and cool until just barely warm.

Make a glaze by mixing together the powdered sugar, lemon rind and enough lemon juice to make a smooth, but not runny glaze. Dip the top side of each cookie into the glaze and decorate with the nonpareils. Let the glaze harden slightly, about 30 minutes, before storing the cookies.

Makes about 30 cookies

VARIATION: Nona sometimes made these cookies without the fig filling. Double the pasty recipe and roll the dough out to about ½" thick. Cut into 1½" squares and bake and glaze as above.

Fragoni

Fragoni, sweetened ricotta enrobed in pastry, is one of Nonna Crocco's luscious baked desserts and one of my favorites. There are many variations of ricotta cheesecake, usually baked like pies or in springform pans. Some do not have a pastry crust but are instead embellished with a crumb crust of amaretti cookies, ground almonds, or bread crumbs.

Nonna's fragoni were none of these but instead, were shaped like large ravioli or baked in pastry cups that she fashioned by pinching the edges of a circle of pastry. Regardless of its shape, fragoni are delicious and in my opinion, beat the typical New York style cheesecake hands down. Nonna's fragoni are one of those desserts you want to eat in big bites so that every single taste bud in you mouth is simultaneously ignited with its goodness.

In addition to Nonna's ravioli shape or pastry cups, fragoni can be baked like other ricotta cheesecakes - in a pie dish, with a crumb crust, or with a regular pie crust. Just be sure that however you make fragoni, you use a good quality ricotta.

Pastry

    4 c. all purpose flour
    4 eggs
    ¾ c sugar
    1 c. sour cream
    ¾ c. butter or margarine
    ½ tsp. salt
    ½ tsp. vanilla extract

Filling

    2 lbs. ricotta
    4 eggs, beaten
    1 c. sugar
    2 tsp. vanilla extract
    ½ tsp. baking powder
    ½ c. golden raisins
    ½ c. chocolate chips
    powdered sugar for serving

To make the pastry, combine the flour, sugar, and salt in a large mixing bowl. Cut in the butter or margarine as with pie crust. In another bowl, whisk together the eggs, sour cream and vanilla extract, then stir into the flour mixture just until the dough comes together. Add a little water or flour if needed to form a soft, but not sticky dough. Form into a disk, wrap in plastic wrap and refrigerate for about 30 minutes.

For the filling, mix (don't beat) the ricotta, eggs, sugar, vanilla and baking powder until well blended. Fold in the raisins and chocolate chips.

To make ravioli shaped fragoni, divide the dough in half and roll out one portion into a more or less square shape about ⅛" thick. Starting at the top of the square, place ¼ cup of the filling in a straight line, an inch apart and about 3 inches from the edge. Take the top edge of the pastry and fold it over the filling. Seal the edge by pressing the dough together with your finger tips. Now, starting at the center, seal the sides by pressing your index finger between the fragoni to seal. Continue towards both ends and push the air out as you work. Make sure all the edges are sealed. Cut the row of fragoni away from the sheet of pastry and then separate by cutting in between. Seal the cut edges with the tines of a fork and place 2" apart on a parchment lined cookie sheet. Continue until all the pastry is used then roll out the other half and repeat.

To make pastry cup shaped fragoni, roll out the dough to about ¼" thick and cut into 6" circles - you can use an inverted bowl as a template. Using your thumb and index finger, pinch about ½" of the edge together, move over to the next ½" and pinch that together, continue all the way around to form a shallow pastry cup. Carefully place on a parchment lined cookie sheet and continue with the remaining dough. Spoon filling just to the top of each cup.

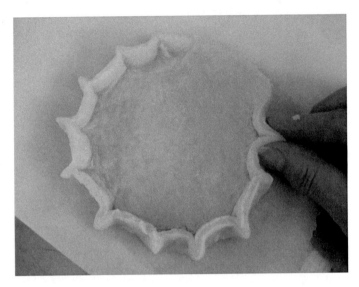

Place in a preheated 350° oven for about 40 minutes until lightly browned and the filling is set. (The pastry cups will spread out as they cook.) Remove from the oven and cool on racks. Dust lightly with powered sugar to serve.

Makes about 10 cup shaped or 24 ravioli shaped

NOTE:
Nonna's fragoni did not include liqueur, but I think the addition of a few tablespoons of amaretto or Grand Marnier would be a nice addition.

To jazz up the presentation, serve with a dollop of whipped cream instead of the powdered sugar.

Filbert and Honey Toasts (Nonna's Hard Cookies)

Nonna Crocco made these delicious and hard cookies that get their distinctive flavor from honey used as the sweetener. They are baked in the same fashion as biscotti and because they are a dry cookie can be stored for several weeks. We ate these cookies dry and crunchy however, they are probably best eaten soaked in coffee or milk. My cousin Lina broke a tooth once biting into one of these cookies!!!

9 c. flour
7 eggs
3 c. honey
5 c. shelled filberts (hazelnuts)
6 tsps. baking powder
2 tsps. baking soda
2 tsps. salt

In a large bowl beat the eggs and then mix in the honey until well blended. Sift together the flour, baking powder, baking soda and salt and combine with the egg-honey mixture. Fold in the filberts until well incorporated.

Divide dough into 4 equal portions and roll each into a log about 3″ in diameter. Place logs on two greased cookie sheets about 3-4″ apart. Bake logs in a 325° oven for 30 minutes or until browned. Remove from the oven and cool slightly. Use a serrated knife and slice the logs crosswise in about ½″ slices. Place the slices on a cookie sheet and return to the oven for about 10-15 minutes turning the slices so that they are toasted and crunchy.

Makes 5-6 dozen

Pignolata (Strufoli)

Pignolata is a pretty and fun to eat dessert that Nonna Crocco made during Christmas. In Italy, desserts and sweets were not part of my family's day-to-day cuisine so the slightly crunchy, honey coated pignolata were a yummy, once a year treat.

A pignolata is assembled from bite-sized nuggets held together with honey. It is a festive addition to any holiday table and eating the pignolata contributes to the holiday's spirit of togetherness as everyone shares the pignolata by pulling away the individual nuggets and popping them in their mouth.

Originally, pignolata was made from pasta dough and it was only the honey that provided additional flavor and sweetness. This recipe caters more to modern tastes with the additional of sugar, leavening and flavoring. Pignolata is supposed to look like a large pine cone so when shaping the pignolata, keep that picture in mind.

> 2 1/2 c. all purpose flour
> 1/2 c. sugar
> 1 tsp. baking powder
> 1 tsp. salt
> 1 egg
> 1/2 c. milk
> 2 Tbl. melted butter or oil
> 1 tsp. vanilla extract
> 1 Tbl. brandy or grappa
> 1 c. honey
> 1 Tbl. multicolored nonpareils
> vegetable oil for frying

In a large bowl combine flour, sugar, baking powder and salt. In another bowl, beat together the egg, milk, butter/oil, vanilla extract and brandy until well blended. Add to the flour mixture, and combine to form a smooth, pliable dough. Working with about ¼ cup of dough at a time, roll the dough into a rope not quite ½" in diameter (about the size of a woman's ring finger). Cut each rope into about ⅜" pieces to create the pignolata nuggets. They should be about as long as they are wide. Repeat with the remaining dough.

Heat a couple inches of oil in a large, heavy skillet to 375°. Working in batches, add the nuggets to the hot oil being careful to not over-crowd. Cook for about 30-40 seconds, stirring carefully and constantly until the nuggets are puffed and golden. Remove the fried nuggets from the oil and drain on paper towels. Repeat until all the nuggets are cooked.

Pour the honey into a sauce pan large enough to hold all the nuggets and heat the honey until viscous and liquified. Remove from heat and stir in the cooked nuggets to evenly coat with honey; cool slightly. Turn onto a large serving platter and with your hands lightly oiled to prevent sticking, press the nuggets together into the shape of a pine cone. While the honey is still slightly warm, sprinkle with the nonpareils. Cool completely or chill in the refrigerator for a few hours before serving.

Makes 8 servings.

VARIATIONS:

- When mixing the cooked nuggets with the honey, add pine nuts or other nuts.
- In addition to the nonpareils, decorate the pignolata with cherries or other dried fruit.
- Flavor with lemon rind or cinnamon instead of vanilla.
- Make small, individual pignolate and serve them in cupcake liners.

Pizzelle

These waffled, crispy cookies are ubiquitous among the Italian community. They can be found on family tables enjoyed with coffee, attractively packaged in Italian markets, given as gifts during Christmas, and at nearly any gathering attended by Italians.

The classic pizzelle baker is a hinged set of round pizzelle irons - similar to waffle irons - with about 3 foot long metal handles extending from the sides opposite the hinge. The pizzelle irons imprint pretty designs on the pizzelle, some are even embossed with the family shield or initial of the family owning the pizzelle baker. To make a pizzelle, a doughy batter is pressed between the irons and the long handles are used to hold the irons over a heat source (like a stove-top or fire) to bake one side of the pizzelle, then flipped, to bake the other.

In typical Nonna Crocco fashion, when she made pizzelle, she made batches of dozens and dozens. It would not be uncommon for her to make 10-15 dozen at a time and sometimes we would go to her house and help bake them. Nonna had a stove in her basement and two pizzelle bakers so while my mom and Nonna worked the pizzelle bakers, my dad would watch the second hand on his watch and call out the precise time to flip the pizzelle bakers and when to remove the pizzelle from the baker (pizzelle cook quickly and are pretty much ruined if over cooked). We kids would help stack the pizzelle and of course, sample them too.

Pizzelle bakers like Nonna's are hard to find since modern pizzelle bakers are electric, whereby simplifying the baking process and allowing for better heat control and therefore, more uniform pizzelle. Palmer makes a nice, two-pizzelle baker.

If stored in a dry place, pizzelle will easily keep for a couple of weeks. My mom stores her's in a paper towel lined cardboard box on top of the refrigerator where the slightly warm air from the compressor keeps the pizzelle nice and crisp. To re-crisp pizzelle, just put them in a single layer on the rack of a warm oven for a few minutes.

Pizzelle can be made in a variety of flavors or with ground nuts replacing some of the flour however, anisette flavor is most traditional. Nonna always used anisette extract but I like using anisette seeds - I like the anisette punch when you bite into one and think their amber specking in the finished pizzelle is pretty.

> 12 eggs
> 3 c. sugar
> 2 c. vegetable oil
> 5 c. flour
> 4-5 tsp. baking powder
> 2-3 Tbl. extract flavoring - anisette, vanilla or almond
> pinch of salt

Whisk the eggs and sugar together in a large bowl. Whisk in the oil until smooth then add the extract flavoring. Combine the flour, baking powder and salt then stir into the oil-sugar-egg mixture in 3 batches, mixing between batches. The texture should be similar to a soft cookie dough.

If time allows, refrigerate the batter over night. In any case, drop the batter by spoonful onto the center of a preheated pizzelle iron. Close the lid and bake for about 40-50 seconds or until the pizzelle are slightly browned. Remove with a fork and lay flat on a kitchen towel to cool. The pizzelle will be pliable as soon as they come off the iron but will become crispy as they cool. Once cool, you can stack the pizzelle.

For variation, substitute 1 cup of flour with 1 cup of ground nuts.

Makes 4-5 doz.

NOTE:
I like butter in cookies so use the following recipe for pizzelle batter and usually make a double or triple batch.

> ½ c. butter
> ⅔ c. sugar
> 3 eggs
> 1¾ c. flour (approximate)
> ½ tsp vanilla extract
> 1 Tbl. anise seed
> 1 tsp. baking powder
> pinch of salt

Cream the butter and sugar. Add eggs, vanilla and anise seed (rub the anise seed between the palms of your hand to release their flavor) mix until smooth. Combine the flour, baking powder and salt then add to the butter-sugar-egg mixture in 3 batches mixing between batches. The texture should be similar to a soft cookie dough.

Drop by spoonful onto center of preheated pizzelle iron. Close lid and bake about 40-50 seconds. Remove with fork and cool.

Makes 1½ doz

Sponge Cake

Sponge Cake was one of my Nonna Crocco's specialties. She had perfected a technique that resulted in consistently light, fluffy and mountainously tall cakes. I'm not sure that anyone else has ever been able to duplicate her precision. This cake is especially good with a cup of fresh coffee, or served with sweetened fresh berries and whipped cream.

9 eggs separated at room temperature
1½ c. flour or cake flour
1½ c. sugar
¼ c. oil
¼ c. water
1 tsp. baking powder
1 tsp. vanilla
1 tsp. cream of tartar

Put the egg whites and cream of tartar in a large bowl and whip until the egg whites are stiff but not dry. In another medium size bowl mix the egg yolks, sugar, vanilla, oil and water until well combined. Sift the flour and baking powder and mix into the egg yolk mixture until just combined. Gently fold the egg whites into the egg yolk mixture one third at a time - do not over mix, otherwise the egg whites will break down and will hinder the cake's lift.

Pour the batter into an un-greased tube pan and place in a 350° preheated oven for 10 minutes. Turn the oven temperature down to 300° and bake for an additional 45 minutes. Remove the cake from the oven and turn the cake upside down and allow to cool completely. If the cake is taller than the "feet" on the tube pan, place the center opening of the tube pan over a bottle.

When cooled, remove the cake from the pan and serve either plain, sprinkled with powdered sugar or drizzled with glaze made with powdered sugar, milk and vanilla. For a lemon glaze, mix powdered sugar, lemon juice and grated lemon rind.

Serves 10-12

Tiramisu

Tiramisu is a classic Italian dessert that we included in our dessert repertoire after it gained popularity in Italian-American cuisine. My mom and I developed this recipe during the Christmas holiday replacing the more common ingredient of rum or marsala with the mocha flavor of Kahlua.

2 c. espresso coffee
½ c. Kahlua
8 egg yolks
1 c. sugar
4 egg whites
1c. whipping cream
1 lb. Mascarpone cheese
2 8-oz. packages cream cheese, softened
½ tsp. vanilla extract
2-3 oz. shaved milk chocolate
16-18 oz. package Savoiardi ladyfingers

To make filling:
In the top of a double boiler, beat the egg yolks and ¼ cup of the sugar until light in color and mixture forms ribbons when dripped from the beater (halfway to zabaglione). Cool for about 5 minutes. Beat the egg whites until stiff and transfer to a large mixing bowl. Whip the whipping cream until soft peaks form and add to the egg whites. With an electric mixer, cream the cooked egg yolks, Mascarpone, cream cheese, remaining ¾ cup sugar and vanilla extract. Fold together with the egg whites and whipping cream.

Assembly:
Mix the espresso and Kahlua in a wide shallow bowl. Dip the ladyfingers, one at a time into the coffee and Kahlua and arrange in a single layer in the bottom of a large baking pan. The ladyfingers should be slightly softened by the coffee, not soaked through. Spread half of the filling over the ladyfingers and sprinkle with half of the shaved chocolate. Repeat with one more layer of dipped ladyfingers and filling. Garnish with remaining shaved chocolate. Chill for at least 8-hours or overnight. Serve with sweetened whipped cream flavored with vanilla extract.

Serves 16-24

Saltasu

Saltasu is the name Nonna Zilioli gave these pastries because when she dropped them into the hot cooking oil they "jump-up" or saltasu. Other common names for this pastry are Crostoli and Angel Wings. Saltasu are light, crispy and shatter into ethereal deliciousness with each bite.

>3 c. all purpose flour
>3 eggs
>¼ c. sugar
>3 Tbl butter, softened
>2 Tbl. brandy
>½ tsp. vanilla extract
>½ tsp. baking soda
>¼ tsp. salt
>vegetable oil for frying
>powdered sugar for dusting

Combine the flour, sugar, baking soda and salt in a large bowl. In a separate bowl, add the eggs, vanilla, brandy and butter, then whisk well. Pour the liquid mixture into the dry and blend together until the dough forms into a ball. The dough should look and feel similar to pasta dough so add some water or flour a tablespoon at a time if needed.

Cover the dough with a damp cloth and allow to rest for about 20 minutes. Once rested, divide the dough into six equal portions. Roll out to about ⅛" thick - you can use a rolling pin but a clever and easy method is to roll out the dough with a pasta machine. In any case, cut the dough into strips about ½" wide and 9" long. To spiff-up the appearance of the finished saltasu, use a ravioli or pastry cutter to cut the strips as it will give the edges a pinking-sheared look. Repeat rolling and cutting with the remaining dough.

In a large heavy skillet, heat several inches of vegetable oil until it is very hot but not smoking. Working with 5-6 strips of dough at a time, tie each one in a loose, open knot and drop into the hot oil - be sure not to crowd the saltasu - and fry until golden brown, then flip and brown the other side. They cook fast so by the time you add the last one in the oil, the first on will be ready to flip. Drain the saltasu on paper towels and while still warm, dust liberally on all sides with the powdered sugar.

When cooled, arrange on a platter and top off with a second dusting of powered sugar. They probably won't last long.

Makes 5-6 dozen

I found my Nonna's hand-written saltasu recipe in an Italian cookbook, *il picolo Talismano della Felicita* that my cousin Laura gave me from my Aunt Teresa's collection. Here is the translation:

This is the Recipe for Saltasu
6 eggs
6 Tbl. sugar
6 Tbl. oil
pinch of salt
1 tsp. vanilla
1 tsp. baking soda
and flour to absorb and to form a ball of dough
but not too hard.

Pull a sheet. Cut in strips. Shape to your liking. Fry in boiling oil until the color of gold. Then, sprinkle with powered sugar.

Qui e il recepy dei dei saltasü.

6. uova
6 chucchiai di zucchero
6 chucchiai di olio.
1 pinch di sale
1 chucchiaino di vanilla
1 chucchiino di Berhin soda
e farina quanto ne assorbe
tanto da formare una pasta
non troppo dura. tirata la sfoglia
si taglia a listelli e si aggiustano
a piacere e si frigge nell'olio
bollente dandogli un colore d'oro
poi si struzza il pauder sugar.

Zuppa Englese

Zuppa Englese is a not too sweet, luscious dessert of layered angel food cake and pastry cream that is laced generously with brandy and liqueur. It should have a good alcohol punch but not so much so that it over powers the overall dessert. The sweetness of the cake and pastry cream should balance well with the brandy and liqueur so you may want to adjust the amount of brandy and liqueur to suit your own taste. It is very important that you allow the Zuppa Englese to chill for a minimum of 24 hours before serving so that the brandy and liqueur can infuse the entire Zuppa Englese.

2 store bought Angel Food cakes
3 c. milk
2 vanilla beans or 1 tsp. vanilla extract
1¼ c. sugar
½ c. all purpose flour
6 to 8 well beaten egg yolks
OR   4 eggs and 4 yolks
½ stick cold butter cut into small pieces
½ c. brandy
⅓ c. total[2] of Kahlua, Grand Marnier and Amaretto
2 tsp. Grenadine
1 pt. whipping cream
½ c. powered sugar
½ tsp. vanilla extract

Make vanilla pasty cream by scalding the milk with the vanilla beans (if using). Mix the sugar, flour and eggs in the top of a double boiler over, not in, boiling water and cream until light. Now remove the vanilla beans and gradually add the scalded milk. Stir until all is well blended, and cook stirring constantly until it just reaches the boiling point and is the consistency of pudding. Remove from the heat and add the cold butter a few pieces at a time and stir to melt. If using vanilla extract, stir into the pastry cream. Mix and cool mixture slightly. Continue to stir to release the steam and prevent crusting.

To assemble the Zuppa Englese, use a fork and pull the Angel Food cake into ¾" slices. Line the bottom of a spring form pan with tightly fitting slices of

---

2   You can use any combination of liqueur(s) that you like

cake.   Sprinkle the cake generously with ½ of the brandy and ½ of each liqueur – the cake should be moist but not soaking. Dot with 1 tsp. Grenadine for color. Cover the cake with ½ of the pastry cream. Repeat the layerings so you have two layers total – you should end with the pastry cream. Cover with plastic wrap and chill thoroughly for at least 24-hours.

To serve, whip the whipping cream, powered sugar and ½ tsp. vanilla extract until stiff peaks form.   Remove the sides of the spring form pan and generously ice the Zuppa Englese with the whipped cream and top with a small amount of shaved chocolate - if desired. Or, serve slices of the Zuppa Englese topped with whipped cream.

Serves 10-12

Beverages

Wine (Vino)

How could a dinner or gathering be truly Italian without at least a few bottles of good vino? This was certainly the case for all of our family get-togethers. In fact, we often bought wine in gallon bottles and served it decanted in glass carafes, placing several on the long dinner tables so that everyone had a carafe of wine within arms reach. Reds were typically the wine of choice although white wines occasionally found their way to the table as well. As kids, we sometimes had wine coolers made by pouring a few tablespoons of red wine in a glass then filling it with Vernor's (Detroit's own brand of ginger ale) or lemon-lime soda like 7-Up. No one ever over-indulged or became inebriated - vino is just what we served at family dinners and to our guests.

In addition to his various farming properties, my great-grandfather, Giovanni Menniti (my Mom's grandfather; Nonna Crocco's father), owned a vineyard from which he made and sold wine as the family's source of cash revenue. He had a reputation as a skilled wine maker and his wines were considered quite good by the locals. Both sets of my grandparents also made wine once they were in the US. This was common among the Italian-American community where the men often engaged in passionate arguments over who's wine was best.   I so clearly remember as a child descending into my Nonna and Nonno's basement to find it filled with stacks of wooden crates bursting with wine grapes (usually Zinfandel) that had been recently purchased at Detroit's produce rail-terminal. Wine making contraptions and wooden barrels filled the spaces between the crates and while the adults busied themselves with crushing grapes, we wandered among the crates sampling the tangy globes.

Wine making is a multi-step process that takes place over several months so, we made multiple trips into Nonna and Nonno's basement, each time moving the fermenting process along until it finally culminated with bottling and corking. Once filled, the dark, green bottles were carefully placed in the wine cellar to age (for his wine cellar, Nonno Crocco converted the room that before gas furnaces, was used to hold the heating coal). My Nonna Zilioli always held a small barrel of wine aside that she further fermented into red wine vinegar. Whenever she, my mom or my aunt needed vinegar, she merely siphoned some into a bottle with a section of rubber tubing that she kept near her vinegar barrel. Back then, grocery stores were not stocked with the huge array of "specialty" vinegars like they are today so thanks to Nonna's understanding of the fermenting process, our family kitchens were always supplied with plenty of red wine vinegar which we used liberally on all sorts of salads.

Once the California wine industry was established, we were able to buy good California wines for less than what it cost to make, so eventually abandoned the practice of making wine; except for my brother, Larry, who in some years still makes a batch. Even though he employs modern wine making techniques using fancy devices to measure the sugar in grapes, and aging wine in glass containers, he does not waver from the spirit and tradition that he first found in our Nonna and Nonno's basement.

Whether a quiet evening alone or any sort of gathering with family and friends, a nice wine is sure to add interest and stimulation.

Aunt Teresa always drank wine coolers - here's how to make one:

> ¼ c. red wine
> 12 oz. ginger ale or lemon-line soda
> ice

Fill a tall glass with ice, add the wine and top off with ginger ale or lemon-lime soda. Enjoy!!!

Coffee

If you were to visit anyone in my family, you can be sure that within minutes of your arrival, they would be brewing a fresh pot of coffee. Coffee was an ever present beverage that accompanied (and still does) countless conversations, celebrations, discussions, and arguments that were held around many a family table. We always served coffee with a bowl of sugar and a creamer of milk or half-and-half as slightly sweetened with half-and-half was always popular. If it were a special occasion (or if my Nonno Zilioli was present), a bottle of whiskey or anisette was also offered for coffee royale.

When we were kids and visited our Nonna, she sometimes treated us with a small cup of coffee sweetened with sugar and mellowed-out with plenty of creamy whole milk. This same coffee preparation is something that when my mom was growing up in Calabria, they often ate for breakfast poured over a bowl of frise (crispy-dried bread). They broke chunks of frise into a bowl, warmed the coffee, sugar and milk in a small pan and then poured it over the frise. The coffee soften the frise and they ate it with a spoon, not unlike a bowl of hot cereal. In fact, I sometimes eat my breakfast flakes or oats-ohs the same way.

Today, the gentrified crowd frequent trendy coffee shops and put out good money for this same coffee drink which is chicly referred to as a "latte". I wonder if they would still think themselves so sophisticated if they realized the latte got its roots from the tables of simple Italian farmers.

You can find many references for the exact ratio of coffee to water, and the precise temperature for brewing the perfect pot of coffee but here are some basics.

> 1-2 tablespoon good quality ground coffee per cup
> always start with fresh, cold water
> if you add dairy to coffee, use half-and-half or cream

Brew a pot of coffee and serve it steaming hot in your favorite mugs. If desired, sweeten with sugar and add half-and-half or cream. For a special treat, add a splash of booze or liqueur. Sit down with people you love and have a conversation.

Tamarindo

My cousins, Laura and David, lived across the street from us and since my Aunt Teresa was a school teacher, she too had summer vacations when we did. Every summer she took us on many outings and adventures but mostly, my cousins, sister, brother and I spent a lot of time together just playing, riding our bikes, or splashing around in the pool. On hot summer days while we were busy with whatever it was we were doing in the backyard, Aunt Teresa

would often step out onto the back porch carrying a big pitcher of freshly made tamarindo. We loved the stuff, and the sight alone was nearly enough to quench our thirst. In tribute to this delicious beverage, my sister and cousin made up a crazy piano tune titled "Tamarindo on the Rocks" whose lyrics repeat "tamarindo on the rocks" over and over.

Tamarindo is a slightly sweet, slightly tart drink made by mixing water and tamarind syrup - a syrup of sugar and refined tamarind pulp. The syrup can be found at Italian and Latin American grocery stores.

> tamarind syrup
> fresh, cold water
> ice
> lemon wedges, optional

Mix the tamarind syrup and water as directed. Fill a glass with ice and pour the tamarindo over the ice. If desired, garnish with a squeeze of lemon. Sit in a shady spot and enjoy.

Italian Cream Sodas

Detroit has a local soda-pop company called Faygo that was very popular when I was growing up. They made a large array of flavors including all the usual ones like - cola, rock-n-rye (aka Dr. Pepper), ginger ale, root beer and a couple fruity ones too, like orange, grape and Red Pop - a non-specific cherry-strawberry-maybe berry flavor (no one really knows the exact flavor of Red Pop). We were not big soda drinkers but did occasionally have soda at dinner. When we had orange, my dad made his version of an Italian cream soda by pouring equal parts orange soda and milk in his glass with ice. This may sound strange but is actually quite good - think creamsicle.

My dad's Italian cream sodas are quick and easy but here is a more sophisticated version using flavored syrups - I like Torani brand syrups - which can be found at import markets or well stocked liquor stores. Use your favorite flavor - fruit flavors are especially good but so are vanilla and almond.

6 oz. club soda
3 oz. whole milk or ½ and ½
1 oz. Torani syrup
whipped cream - optional
ice

Fill a 16 ounce glass about ⅔ with ice. Add the club soda, milk or ½ and ½, and then lace the syrup over the top. If desired, top with some whipped cream. Stir and enjoy.

Cherry Grappa

Nonna Crocco had an Abruzzese lady-friend named Cleria. Cleria was a very rotund, rather slow, plodding woman which was in stark contrast to high-energy, always busy Nonna. Cleria was not exactly the sharpest tack in the box but not wanting to disparage her, I will spare the many examples of why we always wondered why Nonna hung around with her. Just leave to say that Nonno referred to her as "The Balloon".

However, one of the more interesting aspect of Cleria is that she made grappa, a moonshine-like liquor distilled from the stems and grape skins that settle to the bottom of the barrel during wine making. Nonna usually had a

couple bottles of Cleria's grappa and used it to made cherry grappa by "pickling" bing cherries in jars of grappa. When the grappa became cherry flavored, and the cherries became grappa pickled, Nonna served the cherry grappa in shot glasses along with a couple of the cherries and a toothpick for eating them.

My Nonna Zilioli also made cherry grappa and sometimes used prunes instead. Grappa has become a fashionable spirit and can be found at liquor markets however, vodka would be a good substitute. Aunt Teresa made a vodka version using sour cherries and sugar.

> 1½ c. bing cherries, washed and stemmed
> OR 1½ c. frozen sweet cherries
> 1c. grappa

Pack a pint jar with the cherries and fill with grappa to cover the cherries. Close the jar and place in your liquor cabinet for 1 week. When ready, pour a small amount of the cherry grappa in a shot glass or cordial glass, add a couple cherries and serve with a toothpick for eating the cherries.

NOTE: The cherry grappa can be used to make a tasty cocktail called Leonardo Da Vinci by mixing ⅓ cup of the cherry grappa with a couple shakes of angostura bitters and ½ teaspoon sugar in a rocks glass. Add ice, stir and top with a few of the cherries.

Made in the USA
San Bernardino, CA
08 December 2016